Hazrat Pir-o-Murshid Inayat Khan

CARAVAN OF SOULS

CARAVAN OF SOULS

An Introduction to the Sufi Path of
HAZRAT INAYAT KHAN

Compiled and Edited by
PIR ZIA INAYAT-KHAN

Sulūk Press
New Lebanon New York

Published by
OMEGA PUBLICATIONS INC.
New Lebanon NY
www.omegapub.com

Source material in the text courtesy of the International Sufi Movement
Cover heart and wings image courtesy of the Nekbakht Foundation
Cover design by Sandra Lillydahl

This edition is printed on acid-free paper that meets
ANSI standard X39–48.

Inayat-Khan, Zia (1971–)
Caravan of Souls
An Introduction to the Sufi Path of Hazrat Inayat Khan
1.Sufism 2. Inayat Khan, 1882-1926.
I. Inayat-Khan, Zia II.Title

Library of Congress Control Number: 2013946580

Printed and bound in the United States of America

ISBN 978-1-941810-02-6 (cloth)

Contents

Contents

Contents

List of Illustrations

Invocation

Toward the One
The Perfection of Love, Harmony, and Beauty
The Only Being
United with all the Illuminated Souls
Who Form the Embodiment of the Master
The Spirit of Guidance.

INTRODUCTION

The heart's tears are the bells of the caravan
The heart's tears are the traveler's native land

Ghazi ad-Din Khan Nizam

Hazrat Inayat Khan opened a new chapter in Sufi history when he brought Sufism from India to North America and Europe in the early twentieth century. Founded in London in 1918, Hazrat Inayat Khan's Sufi Order represents both a faithful continuation of the fourfold lineage he inherited from his predecessors and a visionary renewal of Sufi thought and practice attuned to the needs of today's world.[1] Hazrat's esoteric teachings provide a potent framework for the transformation of human consciousness, while his exoteric teachings trace a glowing template for the spiritual reconstruction of society.

In Hazrat Inayat Khan's lifetime his Order was active in the United States, Europe, and India. It has since spread further afield. Once contained in a single organization, several groups working along parallel tracks now maintain and transmit its traditions. While these groups vary in their emphasis on the original form of Hazrat's teaching and practice, their common heritage remains a basis of shared spiritual culture. For all who light their candle from his lamp, Hazrat Inayat Khan is *Murshid* (the Guide).

---

1 As a larger umbrella for his work, Hazrat Inayat Khan founded the Sufi Movement in Geneva in 1923.

1

Hazrat Inayat Khan seldom wrote; but he spoke extensively, and pupils took down many of his discourses. From these transcripts a number of books were produced in his lifetime and still more appeared after his passing. Certain lectures and dictations were set aside for internal use and gathered in sets of esoteric papers. In the 1960s the Sufi Movement published a twelve-volume collection of Hazrat's major works, and in the 1980s the Nekbakht Foundation commenced a series of scholarly editions, of which eleven volumes have so far been published.

While Murshid was still living, an English initiate (*mureed*) named Dr. O.C. Gruner compiled a volume to serve as an introduction to the Order. This handy guidebook, entitled *The Way of Illumination*, contains sections on the history and purpose of the Order, "Ten Sufi Thoughts," Sufi terminology, and the meaning of initiation. In its time it fulfilled an important need.

Seeing that a book along the lines of *The Way of Illumination* was needed again, but one that took stock of the last century of Sufi history, Omega Publications asked if I would compile a volume of this kind, and I was happy to agree. *Caravan of Souls* is the fruit of that effort.

In assembling this volume I have drawn from several sources. The published books and unpublished papers of Hazrat Inayat Khan were naturally of primary importance. The *Biography of Pir-o-Murshid Inayat Khan* produced by the Nekbakht Foundation was also a major resource. The archives of the Nekbakht Foundation and the Sufi Order International supplied an abundance of useful documents, pamphlets, and journals. Among contemporaries of Murshid, I have utilized the writings of Nargis Dowland, Sophia Saintsbury-Green, and Huzurnavaz baron van Pallandt. Shrabani Basu, Dr. Sitara Jironet, and Murshid Wali Ali Meyer provided new essays.

As editor, I have applied a light touch, mostly leaving the texts as I found them. I did trim lengthy passages for the reader's convenience. I also edited the spelling of Arabic, Persian, and Urdu words for consistency. I did not, however, attempt to modernize the authors' language in the case of texts written in the early twentieth century. English usage has changed considerably over the last century, and this is most apparent with regard to gender. A hundred years ago it was conventional to denote humanity as "man" and to use the masculine pronoun exclusively when referring to God. Not so today. I trust that readers will understand that Hazrat Inayat Khan's use of the normal language of his day, language in which the "someone" of an example is always male, does not indicate a patriarchal bias in his thought. As we shall see, Hazrat Inayat Khan was, in fact, groundbreaking in his promotion of female leadership.

Numerous friends and colleagues contributed to the preparation of this book in various important ways. Qahira Wirgman generously supplied documentary material on behalf of the Nekbakht Foundation. Yasodhara Lillydahl and Lakshmi Barta-Norton reorganized the archive of the Sufi Order International, enabling me to thumb through cabinets of well-ordered files. As a trustee of Omega Publications, Ms. Lillydahl proofed, designed, and laid out the book. Ophiel van Leer kindly provided the layout for the songs. My uncle Shaikh al-Mashaik Mahmood Khan was a valuable consultant, as was Sharif Graham. Murshid Karimbakhsh Witteveen and Pir Shabda Kahn gave important input from the perspectives of the International Sufi Movement and Sufi Ruhaniat International. I also benefited from consulting Sarida Brown, Devi Tide, and Munawir Mangold. I am grateful to Shrabani Basu, Dr. Sitara Jironet, and Murshid Wali Ali Meyer for the biographies they contributed. Throughout the preparation of the volume, I have been greatly assisted by Wahhab Sheets, Secretary General of the Sufi Order International.

Hazrat Inayat Khan said, "By initiation it is meant that a Sufi prepares himself here on earth to be capable of appreciating the spiritual souls, and unites with them in the brotherhood of initiation on the Path, which may keep him connected with the caravan which is continually journeying toward the goal."[2] The pages that follow cannot do justice to the landscapes of glory that await the seeker of the Infinite, or put into words the blessings of good company on the path. It is enough if they jingle in tune with the bells of the caravan as it advances toward the far horizon.

---

2 *Githa I*, "Spirit Phenomena, The Ascent of the Spirit" (privately distributed).

THE MESSAGE

The Sufi Message
by Hazrat Inayat Khan

The Message is not for one nation, race, or community; it is for the whole of humanity. Its one and only object is to bring about a better understanding between the divided sections of humanity by awakening their consciousness to the fact that humanity is one family. If one person in the family is ill or unhappy, this must certainly cause unhappiness to the whole family. Yet even this is not the most appropriate simile. Humanity is one body, the whole of life being one in its source and in its goal, its beginning and its end. No scientist will deny this. And if part of the body is in pain, sooner or later the whole body is affected; if our finger aches, our body is not free from pain. Thus no nation, race, or community can be considered as a separate part of humanity.

The Sufi Message, therefore, is not for a particular race, nation, or church. It is a call to unite in wisdom. The Sufi Movement is a group of people belonging to different religions, who have not left their religions but who have learned to understand them better, and their love is the love for God and humanity instead of for a particular section of it. The Sufi Movement does not call man away from his belief or church: it calls him to live it. In short, it is a movement intended by God to unite humanity in brotherhood and in wisdom.

The present-day Sufi Movement is a movement of members of different nations and races united together in the ideal of wisdom; they believe that wisdom does not belong to any particular religion or race, but to the human race as a whole. It is a divine property which mankind has inherited, and it is in this realization that the Sufis, in spite of belonging to different nationalities, races, beliefs, and faiths, still unite and work for humanity in the ideal of wisdom.

The tragedy in life comes from the absence of purity. And as pure really means to be natural, the absence of purity means to be far from being natural. Pure water means that no other substance is mixed with it, in other words, that is in its natural condition. Sufism, therefore, is the process of making life natural. One may call this process a religion, a philosophy, a science, or mysticism, whatever one wishes. All the religious teachers who have come to this world at different times, have brought this process of purification in the form of religion. It is not a new process, it is the same ancient process that the wise of all ages have bestowed. If anything new is given in it, it is the form in which it is presented to suit a certain period of the world.

One may perhaps think that by spirituality it is meant that one must learn something which one did not know before, that one must become extraordinarily good, that one must acquire some unusual powers or have experiences of a supernatural kind. None of these things does Sufism promise, although on the path of the Sufi nothing is too wonderful for him. All these things, and even more, are within his reach; yet that is not the Sufi's aim. By the process of Sufism one realizes one's own nature, one's true nature, and thereby one realizes human nature. And by the study of human nature one realizes the nature of life in general.

It is in self-realization that the mystery of the whole of life is centered. It is the remedy of all maladies; it is the secret of success in all walks of life; it is a religion and more than a religion. And at this time, when the whole world is upset, the

Sufi Message conveys to the world the divine Message. What is wrong with humanity today is that it is not itself, and all the misery of the world is caused by this. Therefore nothing can answer the need of humanity save this process of the sages and the wise of all ages, which leads souls to self-realization.

Life, human nature, the nature around us, are all a revelation to a Sufi. This does not mean that a Sufi has no respect for the sacred scriptures revered by humanity. On the contrary, he holds them as sacred as do the followers of those scriptures; but the Sufi says that all scriptures are only different interpretations of that one scripture, which is constantly before us like an open book, if we could only read and understand it.

The Sufi's object of worship is beauty: not only beauty in form and line and color, but beauty in all its aspects, from gross to fine.

What is the moral of the Sufi? The light which guides the Sufi on the path is his own conscience, and harmony is the justification, which guides him onward step by step to his idealized goal. To harmonize with oneself is not sufficient; one must also harmonize with others in thought, speech, and action; that is the attitude of the Sufi.

The highest heaven of the Sufi is his own heart, and that which man generally knows as love, to a Sufi is God. Different people have thought of the deity as the Creator, as the Judge, as the King, as the Supreme Being; but the Sufis call him the Beloved.

What the Sufi strives for is self-realization, and he arrives at this self-realization by means of his divine ideal, his God. By this he touches that truth which is the ultimate goal and the yearning of every soul. It is not only realization; it is a happiness which words cannot explain. It is that peace which is yearned for by every soul.

And how does he attain to it? By practicing the presence of God; by realizing the oneness of the whole being; by continually holding, every moment of the day, consciously or subconsciously, the truth before his vision, in spite of the waves

9

of illusion, which arise incessantly, diverting the glance of man from the absolute truth. And no matter what may be the name of any sect, cult, or creed, so long as the souls are striving towards that object, to a Sufi they are all Sufis. The attitude of the Sufi to all the different religions is one of respect. His religion is the service of humanity, and his only attainment is the realization of truth.[1]

---

1 *The Sufi Message* (London: Barrie and Rockliff, 1963), vol. 9, pp. 248, 262-63, 252-54 (abridged).

Ten Sufi Thoughts
by Hazrat Inayat Khan

There are ten principal Sufi thoughts, which comprise all the important subjects with which the inner life of man is concerned.

I

There is One God, the Eternal, the Only Being; none exists save He.

The God of the Sufi is the God of every creed, and the God of all. Names make no difference to him. Allah, God, *Gott, Dieu, Khuda, Brahma,* or *Bhagwan,* all these names and more are the names of his God; and yet, to him, God is beyond the limitation of name. He sees his God in the sun, in the fire, in the idol which diverse sects worship; and he recognizes Him in all the forms of the universe, yet knowing Him to be beyond all form; God in all, and all in God, He being the Seen and the Unseen, the Only Being. God to the Sufi is not only a religious belief, but also the highest ideal the human mind can conceive.

The Sufi, forgetting the self and aiming at the attainment of the divine ideal, walks constantly all through life in the path of love and light. In God the Sufi sees the perfection of all that is in the reach of man's perception and yet he knows

Him to be above human reach. He looks to Him as the lover to his beloved, and takes all things in life as coming from Him, with perfect resignation. The sacred name of God is to him as medicine to the patient. The divine thought is the compass by which he steers the ship to the shores of immortality. The God-ideal is to the Sufi as a lift by which he raises himself to the eternal goal, the attainment of which is the only purpose of his life.

II

There is One Master, the Guiding Spirit of all Souls, Who constantly leads His followers towards the light.

The Sufi understands that although God is the source of all knowledge, inspiration, and guidance, yet man is the medium through which God chooses to impart His knowledge to the world. He imparts it through one who is a man in the eyes of the world, but God in his consciousness. It is the mature soul that draws blessings from the heavens, and God speaks through that soul. Although the tongue of God is busy speaking through all things, yet in order to speak to the deaf ears of many among us, it is necessary for Him to speak through the lips of man. He has done this all through the history of man, every great teacher of the past having been this Guiding Spirit living the life of God in human guise. In other words, their human guise consists of various coats worn by the same person, who appeared to be different in each. Shiva, Buddha, Rama, Krishna on the one side, Abraham, Moses, Jesus, Muhammad on the other; and many more, known or unknown to history, always one and the same person.

Those who saw the person and knew Him recognized Him in whatever form or guise; those who could only see the coat went astray. To the Sufi, therefore, there is only one teacher, however differently He may be named at different periods of history, and He comes constantly to awaken humanity from the slumber of this life of illusion, and to guide man onwards towards divine perfection. As the Sufi progresses in this view, he recognizes his Master, not only in the holy ones, but in the wise, in the foolish, in the saint and in the sinner, and has never allowed the Master, who is One alone and the only One, who can be and who ever will be, to disappear from his sight.

The Persian word for master is murshid. The Sufi recognizes the murshid in all beings of the world, and is ready to learn from young and old, educated and uneducated, rich and poor, without questioning from whom he learns. Then he begins to see the light of *risalat*, the torch of truth which shines before him in every being and thing in the universe; thus he sees *rasul*, his divine Message bearer, a living identity before him. Thus the Sufi sees the vision of God, the worshipped deity, in His immanence, manifest in nature; and life now becomes for him a perfect revelation both within and without.

It is often for no other reason than clinging to the personality of their particular teacher, claiming for him superiority over other teachers, and degrading a teacher held in the same esteem by others, that people have separated themselves from one another, and caused most of the wars and factions and contentions which history records among the children of God.

What the Spirit of Guidance is can be further explained as follows: as in man there is a faculty for art, music, poetry and science, so in him is the faculty or spirit of guidance. It is better to call it spirit because it is the supreme faculty from which all the others originate. As we see that in every person there is some artistic faculty but not everyone is an artist, as everyone can hum a tune but only one in a thousand is a musician, so every person possesses this faculty in some form and to a limited degree; but the Spirit of Guidance is found among few indeed of the human race.

13

A Sanskrit poet says, "Jewels are stones, but cannot be found everywhere; the sandal tree is a tree, but does not grow in every forest; as there are many elephants, but only one king elephant, so there are human beings all over the world, but the real human being is rarely to be found."

When we arise above faculty and consider the Spirit of Guidance, we shall find that it is consummated in the *bodhisattva*, the spiritual teacher or divine messenger. There is a saying that the reformer is the child of civilization, but the prophet is its father. This spirit has always existed, and must always exist; and in this way, from time to time, the Message of God has been given.

III

There is One Holy Book, the sacred manuscript of nature, the only scripture which can enlighten the reader.

Most people consider as sacred scriptures only certain books or scrolls written by the hand of man and carefully preserved as holy, to be handed down to posterity as divine revelation. Men have fought and disputed over the authenticity of these books, have refused to accept any other book of similar character, and, clinging thus to the book and losing the sense of it, have formed diverse sects. The Sufi has in all ages respected all such books, and has traced in the Vedas, Zend Avesta, Bible, Qur'an, and all other sacred scriptures, the same truth which he reads in the incorruptible manuscript of nature, the only Holy Book, the perfect and living model that teaches the inner law of life: all scriptures before nature's manuscript are as little pools of water before the ocean.

To the eye of the seer every leaf of the tree is a page of the holy book that contains divine revelation, and he is inspired every moment of his life by constantly reading and understanding the holy script of nature.

When man writes, he inscribes characters upon rock, leaf, paper, wood, or steel. When God writes, the characters He writes are living creatures.

It is when the eye of the soul is opened and the sight is keen that the Sufi can read the divine law in the manuscript of nature; and that which the teachers of humanity have taught to their followers was derived by them from the same source. They expressed what little it is possible to express in words, and so they preserved the inner truth when they themselves were no longer there to reveal it.

IV

There is One Religion, the unswerving progress in the right direction towards the ideal, which fulfills the life's purpose of every soul.

Religion in the Sanskrit language is termed *dharma,* which means duty. The duty of every individual is religion. "Every soul is born for a certain purpose, and the light of that purpose is kindled in his soul," says Sa'di. This explains why the Sufi, in his tolerance, allows everyone to have his own path, and does not compare the principles of others with his own but allows freedom of thought to everyone, since he himself is a freethinker.

Religion, in the conception of a Sufi, is the path that leads man towards the attainment of his ideal, worldly as well as heavenly. Sin and virtue, right and wrong, good and bad are not the same in the case of every individual; they are according to his grade of evolution and state of life. Therefore the Sufi concerns himself little with the name of the religion or the place of worship. All places are sacred enough for his worship, and all religions convey to him the religion of his soul. "I saw Thee in the sacred Ka'ba and in the temple of the idol also Thee I saw."

V

There is One Law, the law of reciprocity, which can be observed by a selfless conscience, together with a sense of awakened justice.

Man spends his life in the pursuit of all that seems to him to be profitable for himself and, when so absorbed in self-interest, in time he even loses touch with his own real interest. Man has made laws to suit himself, but they are laws by which he can get the better of another. It is this that he calls justice, and it is only that which is done to him by another that he calls injustice. A peaceful and harmonious life with his fellow men cannot be led until the sense of justice has been awakened in him by a selfless conscience. As the judicial authorities of the world intervene between two persons who are at variance, knowing that they have a right to intervene when the two parties in dispute are blinded by personal interest, so the Almighty Power intervenes in all disputes however small or great.

It is the law of reciprocity which saves man from being exposed to the higher powers, as a considerate man has less chance of being brought before the court. The sense of justice is awakened in a perfectly sober mind, that is, one which is free from the intoxication of youth, strength, power, possession, command, birth, or rank. It seems a net profit when one does not give but takes, or when one gives less and takes more; but, in either case, there is really a greater loss than profit. For every such profit spreads a cover over the sense of justice within, and when many such covers have veiled the sight, man becomes blind even to his own profit. It is like standing in one's own light. "Blind here remains blind in the hereafter."

Although the different religions, in teaching man how to act harmoniously and peacefully with his fellow men, have given out different laws, they all meet in this one truth: do unto others as thou wouldst they should do unto thee. The Sufi, in taking a favor from another, enhances its value; and in accepting what another does to him, he makes allowance.

VI

There is One Brotherhood, the human brotherhood, which unites the children of earth indiscriminately in the Fatherhood of God.

The Sufi understands that the one life emanating from the inner Being is manifested on the surface as the life of variety; and in this world of variety man is the finest manifestation, for he can realize, in his evolution, the oneness of the inner being even in the external existence of variety. But he evolves to this ideal, which is the only purpose of his coming on earth, by uniting himself with another.

Man unites with others in the family tie, which is the first step in his evolution; and yet families in the past have fought with each other, and have taken vengeance upon one another for generations, each considering his cause to be the only true and righteous one. Today man shows his evolution in uniting with his neighbors and fellow citizens, and even developing within himself the spirit of patriotism for his nation. He is greater in this respect than those in the past; and yet men so united nationally have caused the catastrophe of the modern wars, which will be regarded by the coming generations in the same light in which we now regard the family feuds of the past.

There are racial bonds which widen the circle of unity still more, but it has always happened that one race has looked down on the other.

The religious bond shows a still higher ideal. But it has caused diverse sects, which have opposed and despised each other for thousands of years, and have caused endless splits and divisions among men. The germ of separation exists even in such a wide scope for brotherhood, and however widespread the brotherhood may be, it cannot be a perfect one as long as it separates man from man.

The Sufi, realizing this, frees himself from national, racial, and religious boundaries, uniting himself in the human brotherhood, which is devoid of the differences and distinctions of class, caste, creed, race, nation, or religion, and unites mankind in the universal brotherhood.

VII

There is One Moral, the love which springs forth from self-denial and blooms in deeds of beneficence.

There are moral principles taught to mankind by various teachers, by many traditions, one differing from the other, which are like separate drops coming out of the fountain. But when we look at the stream, we find there is but one stream, although it turns into several drops on falling. There are many moral principles, just as many drops fall from one fountain; but there is one stream that is at the source of all, and that is love. It is love that gives birth to hope, patience, endurance, forgiveness, tolerance, and to all moral principles. All deeds of kindness and beneficence take root in the soil of the loving heart. Generosity, charity, adaptability, an accommodating nature, even renunciation, are the offspring of love alone. The great, rare, and chosen beings, who for ages have been looked up to as ideal in the world, are the possessors of hearts kindled with love. All evil and sin come from the lack of love.

People call love blind, but love, in reality, is the light of the sight. The eye can only see the surface; love can see much deeper. All ignorance is the lack of love. As fire, when not kindled, gives only smoke but when kindled, the illuminating flame springs forth, so it is with love. It is blind when undeveloped, but when its fire is kindled, the flame that lights the path of the traveler from mortality to everlasting life springs forth. The secrets of earth and heaven are revealed to the possessor of the loving heart; the lover has gained mastery over himself and others, and he not only communes with God but also unites with Him.

"Hail to thee, then, O love, sweet madness! Thou who healest all our infirmities! Who art the physician of our pride and self-conceit! Who art our Plato and our Galen!" says Rumi.

VIII

There is One Object of Praise, the beauty which uplifts the heart of its worshippers through all aspects from the seen to the unseen.

It is said in the *Hadith*, "God is beautiful, and He loves beauty."

This expresses the truth that man, who inherits the Spirit of God, has beauty in him and loves beauty, although that which is beautiful to one is not beautiful to another. Man cultivates the sense of beauty as he evolves, and prefers the higher aspect of beauty to the lower. But when he has observed the highest vision of beauty in the Unseen, by a gradual evolution from praising the beauty in the seen world, then the entire existence becomes to him one single vision of beauty.

Man has worshipped God, beholding the beauty of sun, moon, stars, and planets. He has worshipped God in plants, in animals. He has recognized God in the beautiful merits of man, and he has, with his perfect view of beauty, found the source of all beauty in the Unseen, from whence all this springs and in Whom all is merged.

The Sufi, realizing this, worships beauty in all its aspects, and sees the face of the Beloved in all that is seen and the Beloved's spirit in the Unseen. So wherever he looks his ideal of worship is before him. "Everywhere I look, I see Thy winning face; everywhere I go, I arrive at Thy dwelling place."

IX

There is One Truth, the true knowledge of our being, within and without, which is the essence of all wisdom.

Hazrat 'Ali says, "Know thyself, and thou shalt know God."

It is the knowledge of self which blooms into the knowledge of God. Self-knowledge answers such problems as: whence have I come? Did I exist before I became conscious of my present existence? If I existed, as what did I exist? As an individual such as I now am, or as a multitude, or as an insect, bird, animal, spirit, jinn, or angel? What happens at death, the change to which every creature is subject? Why do I tarry here awhile? What purpose have I to accomplish here? What is my duty in life? In what does my happiness consist, and what is it that makes my life miserable?

Those whose hearts have been kindled by the light from above begin to ponder such questions, but those whose souls are already illumined by the knowledge of the self understand them. It is they who give to individuals or to the multitudes the benefit of their knowledge, so that even men whose hearts are not yet kindled, and whose souls are not illumined, may be able to walk on the right path that leads to perfection.

This is why people are taught in various languages, in various forms of worship, in various tenets in different parts of the world. It is one and the same truth; it is only seen in diverse aspects appropriate to the people and the time. It is only those who do not understand this who can mock at the faith of another, condemning to hell or destruction those who do not consider their faith to be the only true faith.

The Sufi recognizes the knowledge of self as the essence of all religions; he traces it in every religion, he sees the same truth in each, and therefore he regards all as one. Hence he can realize the saying of Jesus: "I and my Father are one." The difference between creature and Creator remains on his lips, not in his soul. This is what is meant by union with God. It is in reality the dissolving of the false self in the knowledge of the true self, which is divine, eternal, and all-pervading. "He who attaineth union with God, his very self must lose," said Amir.

X

There is One Path, the annihilation of the false ego in the real, which raises the mortal to immortality, in which resides all perfection.

"I passed away into nothingness—I vanished; and lo! I was all living." All who have realized the secret of life understand that life is one, but that it exists in two aspects. First as immortal, all-pervading and silent; and secondly as mortal, active, and manifest in variety. The soul, being of the first aspect, becomes deluded, helpless, and captive by experiencing life in contact with the mind and body, which is of the next aspect. The gratification of the desires of the body and fancies of the mind do not suffice for the purpose of the soul, which is undoubtedly to experience its own phenomena in the seen and the unseen, though its inclination is to be itself and not anything else. When delusion makes it feel that it is helpless, mortal and captive, it finds itself out of place. This is the tragedy of life, which keeps the strong and the weak, the rich and poor, all dissatisfied, constantly looking for something they do not know. The Sufi, realizing this, takes the path of annihilation, and by the guidance of a teacher on the path, finds at the end of this journey that the destination was he. As Iqbal says,

"I wandered in the pursuit of my own self; I was the traveler, and I am the destination."[1]

---

1 *The Sufi Message* (1960), vol. 1, pp. 13-22.

HISTORY

Sufism, East and West

The central idea of Sufism is believed to have existed from the beginning of Creation. Traces of Sufism are to be found in all periods of history, but mostly during the age of Hebrew prophets and ecstatics, who themselves were Sufis.[1]

Sufism was intellectually born in Arabia, devotionally reared in Persia, and spiritually completed in India.

Every incident has its own time, and it has been ordained by the Supreme Will that East and West shall now unite in the call of God, the Lord of both East and West.

Inayat Khan, the pioneer exponent of Sufism and oriental music, arrived in America in 1910, trusting in the injunction of his *pir-o-murshid*, Qutb al-Aqtab Sayyid Muhammad Abu Hashim Madani, who struck the chord of his soul at the right time. He said, when blessing him, "Go thou abroad into the world, harmonize the East and the West with the music of thy soul, spread the knowledge of Sufism; for thou art gifted by Allah, the most Merciful and Compassionate."

Inayat Khan, after some years of steady perseverance, established the Sufi Order in the western world, in America, England, Russia, and France, initiating many disciples. His

---

1 *The Sufi Message* (pamphlet) (London: n.p., n.d.), p. 1.

object in this was to serve humanity by giving the Message of universal brotherhood and by helping seeking souls to unfold toward their Lord, the God of the Universe.[2]

---

2 *Sufi Call* (pamphlet) (London: Sufi Publishing Society, 1916), pp. 5-6 (abridged).

The Silsila Sufian
by Hazrat Inayat Khan

Sufis, who had received spiritual training from all previous prophets and leaders, likewise received training from Muhammad. The openness of Muhammad's essential teachings paved the way for them to come forward before the world without the interference they previously experienced, and a mystic order called the *Sahaba-yi Safa*, Knights of Purity, was inaugurated by the Prophet, and afterwards was carried on by 'Ali and Siddiq. The lives of these knights were extraordinary in their wisdom, piety, bravery, spirituality, and great charity of heart. This Order was carried on by their successors, who were called pir-o-murshid, *shaikh*, etc., one after another, duly connected as links in a chain. The spiritual bond between them is a miraculous force of divine illumination, and is experienced by worthy initiates of the Sufi Order, just as the electric current runs through all connected lamps and lights them. By this means the higher development is attained without great efforts.[1]

---

1 Hazrat Inayat Khan, *The Sufi Message* (London: Barrie and Rockliff, 1962), vol. 5, p. 21.

The Four Schools

Hazrat Inayat Khan's murshid trained him in the traditions of four Sufi lineages and invested him with their legacy. These lineages represent the historical and initiatic heritage of the Order he founded in the West. All four lines originate with the Prophet Muhammad, "the root of all murshids and the fruit of all prophets."[1]

Chishtiyya

Hazrat Sayyid al-Kawnain Muhammad Mustafa
Hazrat Amir al-Mu'minin 'Ali Murtaza
Hazrat Khwaja Hasan Basri
Hazrat Khwaja 'Abd al-Wahid bin Zaid Basri
Hazrat Khwaja Fuzail bin 'Ayaz
Hazrat Khwaja Ibrahim ibn Adham Balkhi
Hazrat Khwaja Huzaifa Mar'ashi
Hazrat Khwaja Hubaira Basri
Hazrat Khwaja Mumshad 'Ulu Dinwari
Hazrat Khwaja Abu Ishaq Shami Chishti
Hazrat Khwaja Ahmad Abdal Chishti
Hazrat Khwaja Muhammad Chishti

---

1 Hazrat Inayat Khan, letter to Rabia Martin dated 27 July 1913.

28

Hazrat Khwaja Nasir ad-Din Yusuf Chishti
Hazrat Khwaja Qutb ad-Din Mawdud Chishti
Hazrat Khwaja Sharif Zindani Chishti
Hazrat Khwaja 'Usman Haruni Chishti
Hazrat Khwaja Mu'in ad-Din Hasan Sijzi-Ajmiri Chishti
Hazrat Khwaja Qutb ad-Din Bakhtiyar Kaki Chishti
Hazrat Khwaja Farid ad-Din Mas'ud Ganj-i Shakar
  Ajhodani Chishti
Hazrat Khwaja Nizam ad-Din Mahbub-i Ilahi Badauni
  Chishti
Hazrat Khwaja Nasir ad-Din Chiragh Dihlavi Chishti
Hazrat Shaikh al-Masha'ikh Kamal ad-Din 'Allama Chishti
Hazrat Shaikh al-Masha'ikh Siraj ad-Din Chishti
Hazrat Shaikh al-Masha'ikh 'Ilm ad-Din Chishti
Hazrat Shaikh al-Masha'ikh Mahmud Rajan Chishti
Hazrat Shaikh al-Masha'ikh Jamal ad-Din Jamman Chishti
Hazrat Shaikh al-Masha'ikh Hasan Muhammad Chishti
Hazrat Shaikh al-Masha'ikh Muhammad Chishti
Hazrat Shaikh al-Masha'ikh Yahya Madani Chishti
Hazrat Shaikh al-Masha'ikh Shah Kalim Allah Jahanabadi
  Chishti
Hazrat Shaikh al-Masha'ikh Nizam ad-Din Aurangabadi
  Chishti
Hazrat Shaikh al-Masha'ikh Maulana Fakhr ad-Din
  Dihlavi Chishti
Hazrat Shaikh al-Masha'ikh Ghulam Qutb ad-Din
  Chishti
Hazrat Shaikh al-Masha'ikh Nasir ad-Din Mahmud Kale-
  Miya Chishti
Hazrat Shaikh al-Masha'ikh Sayyid Muhammad Hasan
  Jili Kalimi Chishti
Hazrat Shaikh al-Masha'ikh Sayyid Muhammad Abu
  Hashim Madani Chishti
Hazrat Shaikh al-Masha'ikh Inayat Khan Chishti

Suhrawardiyya

Hazrat Sayyid al-Kawnain Muhammad Mustafa
Hazrat Amir al-Mu'minin 'Ali Murtaza
Hazrat Khwaja Shaikh Hasan Basri
Hazrat Khwaja Shaikh 'Abd al-Wahid bin Zaid Basri
Hazrat Khwaja Shaikh Fuzail bin 'Ayaz
Hazrat Khwaja Shaikh Ibrahim ibn Adham Balkhi
Hazrat Khwaja Shaikh Shaqiq Balkhi
Hazrat Khwaja Shaikh Hatim-i Asamm
Hazrat Khwaja Shaikh Abu Turab Nakhshabi
Hazrat Khwaja Shaikh Abu 'Umar Istakhri
Hazrat Khwaja Shaikh Abu Muhammad Ja'far Kharraz
Hazrat Khwaja Shaikh Abu 'Abd Allah ibn Khafif
Hazrat Khwaja Shaikh Abu'l-'Abbas Nahawandi
Hazrat Khwaja Shaikh Akhi Farrukh Zanjani
Hazrat Khwaja Shaikh Muhammad bin 'Abd Allah
Hazrat Khwaja Shaikh Wajih ad-Din Abu Hafs Suhrawardi
Hazrat Khwaja Shaikh Ziya' ad-Din Abu'n-Najib
  Suhrawardi
Hazrat Khwaja Shaikh Shihab ad-Din 'Umar Suhrawardi
Hazrat Khwaja Shaikh Lal Shahbaz Qalandar Suhrawardi
Hazrat Khwaja Shaikh Jalal ad-Din Suhrawardi
Hazrat Khwaja Shaikh Baha' ad-Din Zakariya Suhrawardi
Hazrat Khwaja Shaikh Sadr ad-Din Muhammad
  Suhrawardi
Hazrat Khwaja Shaikh Rukn ad-Din Abu'l-Fath
  Suhrawardi
Hazrat Khwaja Shaikh Makhdum-i Jahaniyan Suhrawardi
Hazrat Khwaja Shaikh Sadr ad-Din Raju Qattal
  Suhrawardi
Hazrat Khwaja Shaikh 'Ilm ad-Din Shatibi Suhrawardi
Hazrat Khwaja Shaikh Qazi Qazan Suhrawardi
Hazrat Khwaja Shaikh Mahmud Rajan Suhrawardi
Hazrat Khwaja Shaikh Jamal ad-Din Jamman Suhrawardi

Hazrat Khwaja Shaikh Hasan Muhammad Suhrawardi

Hazrat Khwaja Shaikh Muhammad Suhrawardi

Hazrat Khwaja Shaikh Yahya Madani Suhrawardi

Hazrat Khwaja Shaikh Shah Kalim Allah Jahanabadi
  Suhrawardi

Hazrat Khwaja Shaikh Nizam ad-Din Aurangabadi
  Suhrawardi

Hazrat Khwaja Shaikh Maulana Fakhr ad-Din Dihlavi
  Suhrawardi

Hazrat Khwaja Shaikh Ghulam Qutb ad-Din Suhrawardi

Hazrat Khwaja Shaikh Nasir ad-Din Mahmud Kale-Miya
  Suhrawardi

Hazrat Khwaja Shaikh Sayyid Muhammad Hasan Jili
  Kalimi Suhrawardi

Hazrat Khwaja Shaikh Sayyid Muhammad Abu Hashim
  Madani Suhrawardi

Hazrat Khwaja Shaikh Inayat Khan Suhrawardi

Qadiriyya

Hazrat Sayyid al-Kawnain Muhammad Mustafa

Hazrat Amir al-Mu'minin 'Ali Murtaza

Hazrat Shaikh ash-Shuyukh Hasan Basri

Hazrat Shaikh ash-Shuyukh 'Abd al-Wahid bin Zaid Basri

Hazrat Shaikh ash-Shuyukh Fuzail bin 'Ayaz

Hazrat Shaikh ash-Shuyukh Ibrahim ibn Adham Balkhi

Hazrat Shaikh ash-Shuyukh Shaqiq Balkhi

Hazrat Shaikh ash-Shuyukh Habib 'Ajami

Hazrat Shaikh ash-Shuyukh Da'ud Ta'i

Hazrat Shaikh ash-Shuyukh Ma'ruf Karkhi

Hazrat Shaikh ash-Shuyukh Sari Saqati

Hazrat Shaikh ash-Shuyukh Junaid Baghdadi

Hazrat Shaikh ash-Shuyukh Abu Bakr Shibli

Hazrat Shaikh ash-Shuyukh 'Abd al-'Aziz Tamimi

Hazrat Shaikh ash-Shuyukh Abu'l-Farah Tartusi

Hazrat Shaikh ash-Shuyukh Abu'l-Hasan 'Ali Hankari
Hazrat Shaikh ash-Shuyukh Abu Sa'id Makhzumi
Hazrat Shaikh ash-Shuyukh 'Abd al-Qadir Jilani
Hazrat Shaikh ash-Shuyukh Ziya' ad-Din Abu'n-Najib
   Suhrawardi Qadiri
Hazrat Shaikh ash-Shuyukh Najm ad-Din Kubra Qadiri
Hazrat Shaikh ash-Shuyukh Majd ad-Din Baghdadi
   Qadiri
Hazrat Shaikh ash-Shuyukh Razi ad-Din 'Ali Lala Qadiri
Hazrat Shaikh ash-Shuyukh Jamal ad-Din Jurfani Qadiri
Hazrat Shaikh ash-Shuyukh Nur ad-Din Isfara'ini Qadiri
Hazrat Shaikh ash-Shuyukh 'Ala ad-Daula Simnani
   Qadiri
Hazrat Shaikh ash-Shuyukh Sharaf ad-Din Mahmud
   Qadiri
Hazrat Shaikh ash-Shuyukh Sayyid 'Ali Hamadani Qadiri
Hazrat Shaikh ash-Shuyukh Ishaq Khuttalani Qadiri
Hazrat Shaikh ash-Shuyukh Muhammad Nurbakhsh
   Qadiri
Hazrat Shaikh ash-Shuyukh Muhammad 'Ali Nurbakhsh
   Qadiri
Hazrat Shaikh ash-Shuyukh Muhammad Ghiyas
   Nurbakhsh Qadiri
Hazrat Shaikh ash-Shuyukh Hasan Muhammad Qadiri
Hazrat Shaikh ash-Shuyukh Muhammad Qadiri
Hazrat Shaikh ash-Shuyukh Yahya Madani Qadiri
Hazrat Shaikh ash-Shuyukh Shah Kalim Allah Jahanabadi
   Qadiri
Hazrat Shaikh ash-Shuyukh Nizam ad-Din Aurangabadi
   Qadiri
Hazrat Shaikh ash-Shuyukh Maulana Fakhr ad-Din
   Dihlavi Qadiri
Hazrat Shaikh ash-Shuyukh Ghulam Qutb ad-Din Qadiri
Hazrat Shaikh ash-Shuyukh Nasir ad-Din Mahmud
   Kale-Miya Qadiri

Hazrat Shaikh ash-Shuyukh Sayyid Muhammad Hasan
 Jili Kalimi Qadiri
Hazrat Shaikh ash-Shuyukh Sayyid Muhammad Abu
 Hashim Madani Qadiri
Hazrat Shaikh ash-Shuyukh Inayat Khan Qadiri

Naqshbandiyya

Hazrat Sayyid al-Kawnain Muhammad Mustafa
Hazrat Amir al-Mu'minin Abu Bakr Siddiq
Hazrat Khwaja Salman Farsi
Hazrat Khwaja Qasim bin Muhammad
Hazrat Khwaja Imam Ja'far Sadiq
Hazrat Khwaja Abu Yazid Bistami
Hazrat Khwaja Abu'l-Hasan Kharaqani
Hazrat Khwaja Abu'l-Qasim Gurgani
Hazrat Khwaja 'Ali Farmadi
Hazrat Khwaja Yusuf Hamadani
Hazrat Khwaja 'Abd al-Khaliq Ghijduwani
Hazrat Khwaja 'Arif Rivkirab
Hazrat Khwaja Ashhar Faghnavi
Hazrat Khwaja 'Ali Ramtini
Hazrat Khwaja Muhammad Baba
Hazrat Khwaja Amir Kulal
Hazrat Khwaja Baha' ad-Din Naqshband
Hazrat Khwaja Ya'qub Charkhi Naqshbandi
Hazrat Khwaja 'Ubaid Allah Ahrar Naqshbandi
Hazrat Khwaja Muhammad Qazi Naqshbandi
Hazrat Khwaja Khwajagi Amkunagi Naqshbandi
Hazrat Khwaja Kalan Naqshbandi
Hazrat Khwaja Muhammad Hashim Naqshbandi
Hazrat Khwaja Muhammad Miskin Naqshbandi
Hazrat Khwaja Mir Muhtarim Allah Naqshbandi
Hazrat Khwaja Shah Kalim Allah Naqshbandi

Hazrat Khwaja Nizam ad-Din Aurangabadi Naqshbandi
Hazrat Khwaja Maulana Fakhr ad-Din Dihlavi
  Naqshbandi
Hazrat Khwaja Ghulam Qutb ad-Din Naqshbandi
Hazrat Khwaja Nasir ad-Din Mahmud Kale-Miya
  Naqshbandi
Hazrat Khwaja Sayyid Muhammad Hasan Jili Kalimi
  Naqshbandi
Hazrat Khwaja Sayyid Muhammad Abu Hashim Madani
  Naqshbandi
Hazrat Khwaja Inayat Khan Naqshbandi

Sayyid Abu Hashim Madani

The blessed murshid of our murshid, Inayat Khan, was Sayyid Abu Hashim Madani, who was born in Madras. He was one of the most profound of sages. His sacred remains are near the Purana Pul (old bridge) in the compound of the *dargah* of Miya Paisa at Hyderabad. This man was of a very gentle disposition, soft and kindly, yet inwardly powerful. He had an almost hypnotic ability to purify the minds and hearts of all he contacted through his inner purity and perfection of personality.

One day Inayat Khan and a friend chanced to visit a great sage of Hyderabad, who was a most learned man, Maulana Khair al-Mubin. By a most wonderful coincidence he received a telepathic message, whereupon he called a boy to open the door and prepare a seat, and, turning to his visitors, he said: "Hazrat (Master) is coming."

In a moment there appeared, entering in at the door, a personality which seemed as of one who had dropped from heaven, and was now gently stepping on the earth that was not his place. Yet Inayat felt that the face was not unknown to him. On further thought, it flashed into his mind that it was the same face which he used to see in his meditation. After the master had seated himself in the seat prepared for him, he looked at Inayat and it seemed as if he could not take his eyes away from him.

Their glance meeting awakened in an instant, so to speak, an affinity of thousands of years. "Who is this young man? He attracts my soul very intensely," said the master. Maulana said: "Your Holiness, this young man is a musical genius and is desirous of submitting himself to your most inspiring guidance." The master instantly granted the request and initiated Inayat then and there.

Inayat went as often as he could to see his murshid, who lived at a distance of about seven miles, and he regarded his murshid as one would regard his king. The link between Inayat and his murshid increased every moment of the day. The murshid saw in him his life's purpose, to which even Inayat himself was not yet awakened. Neither did his murshid try to awaken it, except that he prepared him and led him along the road of his destiny, in his most gracious way of mercy and compassion.

After his initiation by the hand of his murshid, Inayat went to the murshid's house for six months, during which not one word was spoken to him by his murshid on metaphysics. An incident of an amusing nature occurred as, for the first time in his life, Inayat heard his murshid's words on metaphysics. He became so keenly interested and filled with enthusiasm about what was being said that he took a notebook from his pocket, intending to take notes of it. But as soon as the murshid saw the pencil and notebook in his hand, he instantly began to speak of an altogether different subject. Inayat realized by this that his murshid meant that his words must be engraved on the soul; they were not to be written with a pencil on the pages of a notebook.

He would return home silent and remain speechless for hours, pondering over the words which had fallen upon his ears. His friends began to wonder what could have happened to him in such a short time, that his whole life should be so changed. He had now become quite a different person in his speech, actions, ways, expression, in his attitude and in his atmosphere. Inayat always remembered the words his murshid said: "There are many ties which make people friends in this world, but there is one tie which is the closest of all, and that is the relation between murshid and mureed, which is a friendship that never ends, for it is in the path of God and truth, and is eternal."

The murshid was fond of music to an unusual degree and greatly enjoyed Inayat's proficiency in music. But with all the great longing he had to hear some music from Inayat, he would never ask him to sing to him; for even that he deemed to be too much of the nature of a command or an intrusion upon Inayat's free will, although he knew that nothing would give Inayat greater pleasure than to carry out his murshid's orders and, especially, to bring him some joy by his music. When he felt a very great longing to hear music, on seeing Inayat he would only say: "Please tell me about that *raga*, what are the notes in it?" Then Inayat would know that his murshid desired to hear music and he would begin to sing in illustration of his explanation. The murshid would be filled with spiritual joy.

The murshid was an ascetic within, but a man of the world without. He had a large family, sons and daughters, and a home where love and culture reigned and which was always hospitably thrown open to all comers. He used to dress simply, in white muslin garments, and sometimes wore a pale yellow turban, which would blend nicely with his white beard. He had a most beautiful, venerable appearance with commanding, lustrous eyes and a spiritual expression radiating, wherever he went, a heavenly atmosphere.

He used to wear shoes embroidered with gold. One day, when Inayat's eyes strayed to these shoes, a thought arose in his mind: why should Murshid, with all his simplicity, wear

37

such costly shoes? At once his conscience pricked him, he felt so guilty that such a thought of one who was above question should have entered his mind, that, instantly, his face turned pale. But the murshid knew all about it and only said with a smile: "The wealth of this earth is only worth being at my feet."

One day, when the murshid was nearing the end of his earthly life, he became rather unwell. It was a heavy burden of sorrow for Inayat to bear, with all his tenderness and sympathy and devotion he had for his murshid. Then the day when the murshid was to depart arrived. On that day, he asked all who were near to come to him and said to them a word of consolation and advice. He next asked for the servants in the house, to bid them farewell and asked all those around him if ever he had spoken a word, or committed a deed that was hurtful, and asked forgiveness of them. Then he prayed for all, gave them blessing, and begged to be left alone in the room where he continued his *zikar;* and through the same zikar he passed from this life of limitation to the sphere of freedom. [1]

---

1 *Biography of Pir-o-Murshid Inayat Khan*, ed. Elise Guillaume-Scham-hart and Munira van Voorst van Beest (London: East-West Publications, 1979), p. 570; pp. 74-81 (abridged).

Hazrat Inayat Khan
by Huzurnavaz baron van Pallandt

Hazrat Inayat Khan was born in Baroda on the 5th July, 1882. His father, Mashaikh Rahmat Khan, came from the Panjab, where he was born in 1843 as a descendant of an ancient family of Sufi saints, *zamindars* (feudal landowners), poets, and musicians. Inayat's mother, Khatija Bi, was the daughter of Shole Khan Maulabakhsh, known all over India as one of the greatest musicians and poets of his time. Born in 1833 at Bhiwani, in the state which is now called Uttar Pradesh, Maulabakhsh travelled widely throughout India and, after a prolonged stay at the court of the maharaja of Mysore, who invested him with princely rank, he settled down in the state of Baroda, which was ruled at that time by the very progressive Maharaja Sayaji Rao Gaekwar, who did so much to raise it to one of the most modern and advanced states in India.

Maulabakhsh took his son-in-law into his household, his *khandan*. This closely-knit family unit grew in importance as the time went by and played a considerable part in the development of cultural, especially musical, life in Baroda. The prominent position of the Maulabakhshi Khandan brought its members outside the narrower Muslim circle and in close contact with leading Brahmin and Parsi families, a circumstance which strongly influenced Inayat Khan's intellectual growth and way of thinking.

All written and oral accounts agree that, even as a child, Inayat had a striking personality, and that various traits seemed to foretell the subsequent course of his development. Extremely lively and bright, his intelligence readily absorbed whatever sufficiently interested him; and he was continually inquiring about God, the nature of things, and points of morality and behavior. And being a scion of the Maulabakhshi Khandan, it is not surprising that, already at an early age, he showed a remarkable proficiency in music. When nine years old, he sang a famous Sanskrit hymn at a court ceremony, which brought him reward from the maharaja and a scholarship. At fourteen he published his first book on music, called *Balasan Gitmala* and written in Hindustani. He started teaching music with so much success that before he was twenty he was made a full professor at Gayanshala, the academy of music founded by his grandfather in 1886, now the Baroda University Faculty of Music.

It was, in a way, his musical achievements which helped to awaken and widen Inayat Khan's spiritual interest; this interest was closely linked to his love for beauty in art and music, for, in his world, cultural and spiritual pursuit went hand in hand. Mehrbakhsh, his cousin, writes in his hitherto unpublished biography: "His parents wondered at times what could be the matter with the child. Very often, in the midst of great activity or excitement among his relatives and friends, Inayat would be very quiet, and he would seem above all things around him." More and more, as he grew up, his search for truth became conscious and consistent.

But before he would find the true purpose of his life, Inayat Khan had still to pass some difficult and sad years. In 1896 Maulabakhsh died, leaving, above all in Inayat's life, a void which none could fill. Then the sudden death in 1900 of his ten years younger brother Karamat Khan made a deep impression on him, and two years later he lost his mother to whom he was devoted. It was after this last bereavement that

Inayat Khan, then aged twenty, started on his first independent journey, leading him to Madras and Mysore, where he
won renown in the same places where his grandfather had
reaped fame and success. He returned to Baroda for about
one year, during which he published an anthology of his
poems in different Indian languages under the title *Sayaji
Garbavali*; but soon it became clear that another scene was
needed for his development and his activities. Steeped as he
was in the Maulabakhshi music and musical concepts, he felt
the urge to carry them to Hyderabad, the principal remaining
center of Mughal tradition and culture at the time. It is prob-
able, however, that he was also aware of the great spiritual
experiences that awaited him there.

The first six months were spent in musical activity and in
making acquaintances and friends; Inayat Khan also wrote
at that time his final book on music, the *Minqar-i Musiqar*,
by which he made his grandfather's musical system available
to Urdu readers. He was then introduced at the court of the
Nizam, H.E.H. Mahbub Ali Khan, who was very mystically
inclined himself and who sensed at once that the musical tal-
ent shown by this young man was but an outer garb covering
some wonderful secret. When, by his questions, he sought
to fathom it, Inayat Khan gave the impressive reply which
Meherbakhsh mentions in his biography. "Huzur," said Inayat,
"as sound is the highest source of manifestation, it is mysterious in itself; and whoever has the knowledge of sound,
he indeed knows the secret of the universe. My music is my
thought, and my thought is my emotion. The deeper I dive
into the ocean of feeling, the more beautiful are the pearls I
bring forth in the form of melodies. Thus my music creates
feeling within me before others feel it. My music is my religion, and therefore worldly success will never be a fit price
for it; my sole object is to achieve perfection.... What I have
brought you is not only music merely to entertain, but the ap-
peal of harmony, which unites souls in God." The musician

had already grown into the Sufi *pir*, and yet he had still to find his murshid; his esoteric training was yet to begin!

Although Inayat Khan had by now received much recognition throughout the whole of India, his attention and interest were more and more drawn towards the spiritual life, towards the mysticism so intimately connected with his music. He found a great friend and guide in Maulana Hashimi, a well-known scholar, who taught him Persian and Arabic literature and, being a mystic himself, recognized in Inayat what other friends of his were at a loss to understand. As Meherbakhsh says, "Hashimi knew that something was being prepared in Inayat for the years that were in store for him, which was beyond words or imagination."

It was in Hashimi's house that Inayat Khan met his murshid, by whose help he was to reach the fulfilment of his stay in Hyderabad. Sayyid Muhammad Hashim Madani was, like Maulana Hashimi and many other leading Hyderabadi Muslims, of Arabic descent, but he was a pir of the specifically Indian Chishti order of Sufis. For four years, until his murshid's death in 1908, Inayat Khan remained in Hyderabad as his enraptured disciple, apart from occasional visits to Baroda. Some of the poems he composed and sang in honor of his murshid have been preserved.

Years later Hazrat Inayat was to devote many of his most beautiful teachings to the relationship between murshid and mureed, and these reflect his recollection of the profound joy and exaltation he himself had found in this relationship. The great process of the spiritual life, that of *fana* and *baqa*, which are the Sufi terms for annihilation and resurrection, of losing the ego and discovering the essence of being, was now becoming a reality to Inayat Khan.

Inayat Khan's remaining years in India were again marked by extensive travels, during which he went to Ceylon, and from there to Rangoon. He and his brothers then went to Calcutta where, apart from a short visit to Baroda rendered necessary by his father's death, they stayed until their departure for the West. This period was the culmination of his life in India; his music and his mysticism were jointly maturing to a rare perfection. But soon his life took another decisive turn; the western world was to be the scene of his future work.

Thus we return to the time so vividly described by Hazrat Inayat in the passage quoted above. Going from one extreme to another, Inayat travelled from feudal India straight to the modern world of the United States. He was accompanied by his five years younger brother, Maheboob Khan, and his cousin and life-long companion, Mohammed Ali Khan, both of whom had given up their promising musical careers in order to remain close to Inayat Khan, whom they considered not only as their brother but as their master on the spiritual path. Later they were joined by their younger brother, Musharaff Khan, six months after they had arrived in the United States.

In 1912 Inayat Khan and his brothers left the New World and travelled extensively through Europe, where they were well received, especially in France and Russia. On their return from the latter country they first settled in France, but left for London in 1914, where they were to remain until 1920.

During the initial period of his stay in the West, Hazrat Inayat Khan's main occupation was, according to his memoirs, to study the psychology and the general conditions there. With his brothers he gave concerts of Indian music, on which he also gave many lectures. Apart from a livelihood, this provided him with an opportunity of developing the spiritual side of his subject and, thus, the esoteric teachings of Sufi mysticism.

In the course of time he initiated a number of mureeds here and there, but it was in England that the first systematic forms were given to the extending activities. By then Sufis were scattered throughout several widely separated countries, and Inayat Khan felt that, in order to weld them closer together, he should use his enforced long stay at one place, during the war period, to develop a more regular pattern. Thus the Sufi Order came into being as an organized entity, comprising a *khankah* or headquarters and National Societies for the different countries. Its activities consisted in the training of the mureeds, the Sufi initiates, while concerts and other public activities took place; and lectures about Sufism as an universal ideal were given, as well as courses for candidates.

In 1912 Hazrat Inayat Khan had married Miss Ora Ray Baker, later Ameena Begum, who bore him four children. In 1920 the family moved to France. Though it was his intention to settle eventually in Geneva, where he wished to establish the headquarters of the expanding Sufi Movement, his family preferred to remain living near Paris rather than moving to Switzerland. Consequently the Sufi Headquarters were organized at Geneva, from whence all Sufi affairs are conducted, while Inayat Khan's private residence remained at Suresnes, on the outskirts of Paris.

As his fame and obligations increased, the extent and frequency of Inayat Khan's travels throughout Europe and the United States grew in proportion; it was only during the summer months that he could return to his residence for any length of time. At first this was intended to be a period of retirement and quiet meditation, but soon the fact of his being available and comparatively free drew to his home a number of mureeds. Hazrat Inayat Khan lectured to them, instructed them individually, and was at all times ready for everyone seeking his help or the comfort of his presence. Thus out of original retirement grew the summer school, soon the busiest and most popular of Sufi activities, and the focal point of Hazrat Inayat's Sufi teaching. The greater part of his later discourses were delivered at the summer school, held regularly from 1921 to 1926; the first year at Wissous, near Paris; then in 1922 at Katwijk, Holland; and subsequently at Suresnes.

This period marks the culmination of his activities. The concentration and unsparing intensity with which he developed his work in different fields seemed unlimited. It was not in the least exceptional for him to lecture on different subjects, three times a day; in addition, every free moment was devoted to receiving, advising, and helping mureeds individually, and to directing the Sufi organizations and their varied activities.

After the closing of what was to be the last summer school under his guidance, Hazrat Inayat Khan left for India in October 1926, accompanied only by his secretary, and arrived at Delhi in the first days of November. His fame had already preceded him, and he was continually urged to lecture and to give instruction. Early in 1927 he went once more to Ajmer, to revisit there the most celebrated of Indian Sufi shrines, the tomb of Khwaja Mu'in ad-Din Chishti; and again he experienced a deep joy in the marvellous serenity and the sacred *sama'* music of this holy place. It was the fatal cold he contracted on this journey which caused his death on the 5th February, 1927, at Tilak Lodge, Delhi, where he was staying.[1]

---

1 *The Sufi Message and the Sufi Movement* (London: Barrie & Rockliff, 1964), pp. 5-11. The "cold" from which Hazrat Inayat Khan died is generally held to have been pneumonia.

Stories of Murshid

The disciple was travelling with him, and together they had left the home of a member of his followers in which there had been an atmosphere more than usually congenial to his way of life and thought. He had been calmly cheerful when the journey began, looking untired and untroubled, young, buoyant, almost gay. During the journey of an hour he talked with the pupil, discussing a book he was writing and plans for the work at the place to which they were going. Suddenly, he broke off in the midst of a sentence and, leaning forward, gazed earnestly from the window at the flying fields, with an expression of deepest pain and sorrow changing every line and muscle of his face; and, as the disciple saw with amazement, his hair becoming grey at the temples.

The plan arranged was not followed when the station was reached, for the Master, scarcely hearing what the disciple said, made a gesture of farewell and moved away among the crowd. The change from a young, upright and manly form was so extraordinary that the pupil stood, dazed and wondering, to watch the bent figure of an old man, bowed beneath some mysterious burden of sorrow, as it disappeared from view. No explanation of this unusual occurrence was given then or afterwards, and when the Master took his class a few hours later, he had again assumed his normal appearance.

Two years later the disciple witnessed a similar change, which took place when the Master was holding a class for his immediate circle of pupils, and which was observed by them all. Among themselves they spoke of it when the class was over, and one of them said, "It seemed as if he were torn by some cosmic agony." The hour of the class was three o'clock in the afternoon; at seven the same day, telegrams in the evening papers gave the first notices of the great and terrible earthquake in Japan.[1]

In many ways, and by small, apparently unconscious acts, the Master gave evidence of the power that was his; one such occurs to the mind of the disciple now. It was unusual for him to speak much when walking but, on this occasion, he had been sitting for an hour or more in Regent's Park and, on leaving, continued his discourse as he paced slowly, the disciple at his side. On reaching the crossroads by Baker Street Station, the Master, without pausing or altering for an instant the rhythm of his walk, stepped off the pavement into the stream of traffic. Alarmed for his safety, in spite of faith in all he did, the pupil followed, and with the same slow pacing step they crossed the double lines of swiftly moving vehicles.

Once only the Master raised his hand, and vividly the disciple remembers the words heard while a plunging dray-horse touches with its head the calm, unhurried form: "And I tell you, my mureed, that every thing which has praise from the world is unnoticed in heaven, and everything which is unnoticed by the world is kept in heaven." They move on between the wheels and through the maze of human endeavour; and, once again, it seems to the heart of the pupil that a great silence falls upon the world. [2]

The scene—a little village on the coast of Holland, then but a collection of fishermen's huts at one end of the beach

---

1 Sophia Saintsbury-Green, *Memories of Hazrat Inayat Khan* (London: Rider & Co., n.d.), pp. 46-48.
2 Ibid, pp. 65-66.

and, at the other, a few hotels open for summer visitors, but at that season closed and silent. The Master is staying at the house of one of his disciples, and the writer of these memories is also there. The wide windows of the studio in which he taught look west across the grey autumn sea, and, all around, the wastes of sand dunes catch and hold the eye with their suggestion of distance from civilization and its importunate desires.

Peace. Silence. With the ocean awash at its gates, the ordered rhythm that was his atmosphere and in which he tuned the broken human chords to harmony with God—all this and more formed, as it were, a web of mystery and beauty in which his pupils moved, as in a dream, throughout the tranquil stillness of the fading year. Always his serenity was the setting of their days, his calm the benison that touched their nights with peace; his humor, like the sun upon the sea, playing with all their passing waves of thought.

And then—a day when, without warning, that most wonderful rhythm trembled upon itself and broke. A strange restlessness took its place, and, during breakfast, the Master neither spoke nor touched the food upon his plate. The morning passed as usual, but those grouped around him saw that his thoughts were far away. His sentences were left unfinished, his movements showed a restlessness altogether new to them. At lunch again, he neither spoke nor ate; but on rising from the table he asked his host and the disciple who writes to accompany him for a walk. They hasten to fetch their coats, but, quick as they are, his impatience is evident; he is waiting at the door and, as they appear, walks hurriedly inland toward the wastes of sand.

Faster he walks, with a gait so unlike his measured steps that they glance at one another in surprise; and soon it is only by almost running that they are able to keep close to him as he goes. After some ten minutes walk they reach the dunes, and there the Master stops; imperiously, and in a voice they scarcely know, he bids them wait till he returns, and, awe-struck by his manner, they obey in silence.

The spot in which he leaves them is a little mound on which a flagstaff has been fixed; and from it the two who wait can see the Master's figure as he walks rapidly, in long strides, planting his stick before him in the shifting sand. He is bareheaded, and his hair, usually so expressive of his love of beauty, is all dishevelled and streams out upon the wind. His garment, a long black cassock and overcloak, adds to the impression of some prophet of old, and involuntarily the disciples utter the same word: "Elijah!" How is it that we *know* he looked like that?

His haste does not impair the sense of majesty and power that comes to them as they watch that figure while it seems to grow larger instead of smaller in the distance, until some quarter of a mile away it disappears among the further dunes. For perhaps three-quarters of an hour they wait in silence which is like a prayer, and then they see him come, not by the path by which he went in urgent haste, but slowly and with measured steps, his aspect of such beauty that they catch their breath.

Gently he treads the narrow sandy way and, as he comes, he stoops to gather flowers, the wild and hardy poppies of the sea, the thistle and the yellow spikes of gorse. His form is slender now and full of grace, his hair is smooth upon his brow; he smiles the heavenly smile that wins their hearts, and, bending, lays the flowers in the pupil's hands. He talks of usual matters on the homeward way, and lightly touches each in humorous vein; no word is said, no question asked that can refer to that strange hour; and so, their hearts alight with joy, they reach the house. Only at supper, which is always a sacrament of peace, he speaks of what has passed. His host is asked if he can find the spot, a tiny basin, green and fresh with grass, behind the mount near which the Master disappeared. "For from today it shall be given the name *Murad*

Hasil, the Mount of Blessing, and those who pray for blessings there shall have their wish granted." So spoke the Master, and no more; but in their hearts the two disciples thought: "It is the place of tryst; he kept it there—with Whom?"[3]

In many ways and at all times it would seem that nature, so much beloved by him, could offer recognition and homage to the Master when human eyes were blinded by preconceived ideas and man-made theologia of the past. On another occasion, when walking with the Master in a forest, the disciple saw a strange phenomenon: a small whirlwind gathers the dead leaves into a spiral form, which raises itself before him some five feet in height and three feet round at the base. At the time, the forest is held in the golden stillness of October, when, if but a leaf falls, it spins slowly through the motionless air to join its fellows in the untroubled quietude of death. Yet, for some three minutes, the miniature vortex whirls and twists in the Master's path, as if moved by a cyclone, to subside again into the utter stillness which hushed the dreaming trees to their last sleep. Later, the disciple asks the Master what such a strange occurrence can mean, and is told "it was an initiation," yet knows that no further question must be put.[4]

A mureed of my acquaintance told me that before he became a mureed he said to Murshid, "Murshid, you want to accept me as your pupil, but you don't know how wicked I am." Murshid answered, "It does not matter." "Yes, Murshid, but I really am a great sinner." Murshid again said, "It does not matter." But the man felt tormented and depressed, and resumed, "But Murshid, you don't know how wicked I am." Whereupon Murshid asked, "Do you love me?" "Certainly; oh, certainly, Murshid." "Do you believe I love you?" Murshid asked. "Yes, certainly, Murshid." "Then," Murshid continued, "then it does not matter."

---

3 Ibid, pp. 72-77.
4 Ibid, pp. 88-89.

But another mureed told me the following: he came to Murshid to be initiated, and he felt the need to confess, before becoming a mureed, that he had sometimes done things that were not quite right. He thought, "It will be sufficient if I just mention the fact; then Murshid is sure to accept and initiate me." But Murshid said, "Indeed! Tell me how it happened." And the candidate mureed had to tell him. Every time he wanted to dispatch the matter and pass it lightly, Murshid kept on asking him and wanted to know every detail till nothing was kept hidden; the man's forehead was all perspiration. He asked, "Murshid, now I suppose you won't accept me as your pupil, will you?" The expression on Murshid's face changed, and with a radiant smile he said, "Yes, now I will."[5]

Murshid and I sat in a train compartment, and he gave me initiation and practices quite openly. Everybody in the train compartment looked as if they didn't even see us. The train conductor came running in and said, "Oh, you are in the wrong train. This train is going to so and so. You should be in the other train, in the platform over there." In order to reach it we had to run, and Murshid ran very well. On the way we met the conductor who had given us the wrong information. I was about to tell him, "You gave us..." But before I could say anything, Murshid said, "Oh, hello, I haven't had so much fun for a long time." [6]

During the war of 1914–18, Murshid lived in London. He used to spend hours in his room meditating in the evenings. Somehow Murshid drew the attention of the police, who wanted to know what this Indian was up to in these days of war. One evening there was a ring at his house. Two policemen told Musharaff Khan, who answered the door, that

5 *Memories of Murshid* (privately distributed), p. 71.
6 Shamcher Bryn Beorse, "Some Memories of Murshid," *The Message*, vol. 7, no. 2, p. 15.

they wanted to search Murshid's room. Musharaff Khan said this was impossible, for on no account did he want to disturb Murshid in his meditations. This, however, made the case even more suspicious, and the policemen said they must be shown into the room.

At his wit's end, Musharaff knocked long at Murshid's door, and, in the meantime, the policemen grew more and more suspicious. At last Musharaff entered Murshid's room, apologized greatly for having to disturb him, and told about the policemen. "Let them come in," Murshid said, rising to his full height.

When the policemen came in and saw Murshid's great majesty, and felt the wonderful atmosphere of the room in which Murshid had meditated all that time, the expression on their faces changed completely. They just looked about the room, as was their duty, then went to Murshid. One of them said, "Master, forgive us; we had our orders." They bowed their heads to him, and Murshid laid his hands upon their heads and blessed them. Then they kissed Murshid's hand and left, full of reverence and deeply impressed.[7]

Years after Inayat's death a Dutch journalist was brought to a pub in Paris, and among the regulars—the usual misunderstood poet and a tragic girl—he met a man who was known as the Heavenly Grape. In almost perpetual drunkenness he preached, all day long, the words of his "great and only friend Inayat Khan." If anybody was desperate or irritable, if he himself climbed a chair to make some sublime statement and fell off in the progress, if one of the regulars wanted to bash him on the head, or if a visitor was surprised at his sermons from the gutter, he could always quote a relevant and authentic saying of "his incomparable master" Inayat. This drunken apostle, according to his own story, had

---

7 Ibid, p. 73.

been a dock laborer in Marseilles. After an accident, Inayat had found and cured him, and then, supposedly, delegated him to the darkest part of Paris. [8]

---

8 Elisabeth de Jong-Keesing, *Inayat Khan: A Biography* (The Hague: East-West Publications, 1974), pp. 175-76.

The Brothers
by Dr. Sitara Jironet

Hazrat Inayat Khan did not walk alone. He reached the West with his brother Maheboob Khan and cousin (or, to use the Indian term, "cousin-brother") Ali Khan, and was later joined by his youngest brother Musharaff Khan. After his passing, it was these three who went on to serve as heads of the Sufi Movement, one after the other.

Shaikh-ul-Mashaikh Maheboob Khan

Maheboob Khan (1887–1948) was five years younger than his brother Inayat Khan. He was born in Baroda in the house of Maulabakhsh. Maheboob was the favorite son of his father, Mashaikh Rahmat Khan. Rahmat Khan stressed simplicity and dignity, and taught his sons to control their emotions and conceal their feelings. Gentle and sensitive by nature, Maheboob Khan practiced austere self-control throughout his life. His inner fortitude was tested and strengthened when, at the age of nine, he experienced a long period of near-paralysis due to illness.

Inayat and Maheboob attended the Gayanshala, the music academy founded by their grandfather, and received thorough training in classical Indian music. Maheboob, however, was very attracted to the music of the West, and avidly pursued it. In time he was invited to conduct Baroda's military bands and the Gaekwar's orchestra, and became a much-sought music tutor among the leading families of the state.

Perhaps the most outstanding quality of Maheboob's musicianship was his voice, which was universally lauded as extraordinarily beautiful. Murshid said of it, "I have never heard, if I were to give my candid opinion, such a voice, saturated with sweetness and rich with beauty, with piercing quality, in the eastern or western part of the world, all my life; and his singing often reminded me of the voice of my grandfather, Maulabakhsh, and yet Maheboob Khan's voice seemed to me even superior."[1]

Maheboob's shyness generally prevented him from singing in public. It was difficult even for his brothers to hear him sing, because as soon as Maheboob noticed anyone listening, he immediately stopped. Murshid had to hide if he wanted to hear Maheboob sing.

Maheboob Khan accompanied Inayat Khan to the West in 1910, leaving behind a newly wedded wife and a promising career. From the day of their departure until Murshid's return to India sixteen years later, Maheboob Khan lived and worked with his elder brother almost continuously. Much of their time was spent travelling. Along with their musical activities, their shared meditations provided continuity over the years.

Life in the West only accentuated Maheboob Khan's reserved and withdrawn personality. Yet in spite of his reluctance to perform in front of an audience, and particularly an audience unable to understand his music, Maheboob Khan succeeded in establishing himself as a respected musician in Europe, and earned admiration for his compositions. Some twenty-five of these compositions were settings of poems by Murshid.

---

1 *Biography of Pir-o-Murshid Inayat Khan*, p. 351.

In 1927 Maheboob Khan reluctantly assumed the role of head of the Sufi Movement, a position he was to hold for more than two decades. He adopted a discreet style of leadership, and answered the demands of the time with quiet perseverance.

Loath to regard himself as the successor to Inayat Khan, Maheboob Khan did not take the title of pir-o-murshid, but chose instead to be called *shaikh-ul-mashaikh*. Although this designation was the equivalent of pir-o-murshid in the by-laws of the Sufi Order, it carried a different resonance for the mureeds.

Maheboob Khan took the view that Murshid had said all that there was to be said. He saw it as his task, therefore, not to add anything new, but to inspire mureeds to study, practice, and live the Sufi Message. His unassuming manner effectively focused mureeds' attention on Murshid's teachings and protected him from undesired exposure.

Maheboob Khan led the three-month summer school in Suresnes each year from 1927 to 1939. During this period the summer school went on much as it had in Murshid's time. Maheboob Khan continued the established tradition, always placing special emphasis on its inner dimension.

Maheboob Khan died unexpectedly at home in The Hague at the age of sixty-one. The cause of death was heart failure. His last words, spoken to Ali Khan in Hindustani, were characteristically understated: "Mulla, I seem to be quite perspiring."

In addition to the impress of a wise and subtle personality, Maheboob Khan's abiding contribution to Sufism is his *oeuvre* of Sufi songs, which has proven perennially inspiring to large circles of mureeds and lovers of music.

Pir-o-Murshid Mohammed Ali Khan

Mohammed Ali Khan (1881–1958) was the cousin of Inayat Khan. Born in the same house just a year apart, Ali

Khan and Inayat Khan grew very close. Throughout his life, Ali Khan remained a strong and loyal companion to Murshid.

Ali Khan's father was an officer serving in the state force. His mother was a daughter of Maulabakhsh's sister. She came from Tonk but moved to Baroda after marriage. Ali Khan was their first child. When he was five or six, Ali Khan's mother and father passed away, one after the other. He was then adopted by his maternal grandparents and taken to Tonk, where he was raised to be the heir of the family's extensive properties.

Ali Khan lived in Tonk for a decade, receiving a traditional madrasa education. A devoted student of the Qur'an and Hadith, he came to be seen as a mulla, or religious preceptor. During these years, Ali Khan also learned the duties of a *jagirdar*, or feudal landowner. With his grandfather, he made rounds of the family estates on horseback, and attended court functions accoutered with sword and shield. Throughout his life, Ali Khan's disposition remained distinctly religious and ceremonial.

At the age of fifteen, Ali Khan moved back to Baroda. In addition to musical studies, he commenced a regimen of physical and spiritual education with a reputed teacher popularly known as Bhayaji. Bhayaji's course of instruction, which included both religious and athletic exercises, consumed most of Ali Khan's waking hours. The result was deepening purity of body, mind, and heart, all of which prepared Ali Khan to become a masterful healer. Bhayaji confirmed his satisfaction in Ali Khan's progress by issuing him an *ijazat*, or certificate of authorization.

When Inayat Khan called Ali Khan to come with him to the West, he readily agreed, though it meant abandoning his estates in Tonk. Over the decades he remained staunchly loyal to Murshid and Maheboob Khan. At the age of sixty-seven, he assumed the leadership of the Sufi Movement.

A mureed's recollection of her interview with him in London in 1950 conveys a sense of how he worked as an instrument of the Spirit of Guidance:

"The room was small and drab, and looked out over a dingy and noisy street. It could hardly have been a less inspiring setting; yet the room will always remain a symbol of the Divine Presence even in the densest matter. Murshid Ali Khan's words, atmosphere and whole being were of God, and the dreary hotel room became a paradise. The first interview ...was like a meditation spoken in a low voice, which was sometimes almost drowned by passing traffic...his words flowed twice into singing, and there was also healing given, and a deep silence; but one could not divide the one part from another. The singing was a revelation of the profoundest devotion of the heart to its Lord, and one realized that one had been brought into the very antechamber of God.... When Murshid Ali Khan broke off to sing during the interview, it was not breaking at all; it was flowing on from what he'd been saying, and it was all a conversation with God containing thankfulness, praise, opening of the heart, too, in sorrow and pain and joy—almost using God as a friend—using the pain and praise as language, as music."[2]

By being in contact with his own thoughts and feelings, with his prayerful attitude to life, Ali Khan seemed always to be fully himself. In his presence mureeds became aware of their own being, reflected back to them through him. As a singer, Ali Khan tuned his listeners with sound waves, turning Murshid's poems and Maheboob Khan's music into a three-dimensional reality by the power of his renderings.

Ali Khan was known as a great healer. There are numerous accounts of how he successfully healed patients whom medical doctors had given up on. He cured not only people suffering from physical ailments, but also sufferers from

---

2 Interview with Roshan Mackail, 1995.

depression, psychological problems, and alcoholism. Ali Khan moreover healed, or purified, rooms, houses and places, as well as relationships between people. There are examples of how he made broken things work instantly, like a car or a door. The secret of his healing power lay in his conviction that he was simply a channel for the divine healing power.

Whereas Maheboob Khan's leadership style was diplomatic, Ali Khan's approach was outspoken. His firm and uncompromising stance was founded on his belief in spiritual hierarchy as an instrument for divine guidance, and purity as a condition for mystical attainment.

At the age of seventy-seven, Ali Khan passed away while doing the zikar in a hospital room. Born and raised in India, he had spent most of his life in the West. Throughout his life he remained devoted to God, to Murshid, and to Sufism.

Pir-o-Murshid Musharaff Khan

Musharaff Khan (1895–1967), too, was born at the house of Maulabakhsh and grew up with his three elder brothers, Inayat, Maheboob, and Karamat. His childhood and early youth were overshadowed by the deaths of several of those who were closest to him. His brother Karamat and mother, Khatija Bi, both died when he was five, and the aunt who afterward looked after him died a few years later. His father, Rahmat Khan, died when Musharaff was thirteen. Musharaff found solace in music and in the pleasure of communing with animals.

Having studied music for a time with his uncle Murtuza Khan, at the age of fourteen Musharaff moved to Calcutta to live and study with Inayat Khan. He grew fascinated by Inayat Khan's asceticism, gazing with awe at the ethereality of his brother's face when he prayed and meditated in the night. Noticing Musharaff's curiosity, Inayat altered his schedule so as not to be observed in his devotions.

When Inayat Khan undertook to travel to the West, he left Musharaff in Calcutta with the promise that he would call him soon. Two years later the summons came. Arriving in New York in February, Musharaff was bewildered by the frigid wind, slippery pavement, and rushing traffic. This was the beginning of a long transition to a new way of life. Musharaff was delighted to be reunited with his brothers, and to accompany them in their musical performances. At the same time, he was slow to acclimate to the West, and suffered from homesickness. Murshida Sophia wrote, "Of Musharaff Khan ... it may be said that he is almost entirely of the East."[3]

Musharaff Khan was sixty-two when he became head of the Sufi Movement following Pir-o-Murshid Ali Khan's passing. His leadership style was not so subtle as that of Maheboob Khan, nor so forceful as that of Ali Khan. But Musharaff had gifts of his own. Musharaff Khan's teachings were simple, inspired, and to the point, and in this he resembled Inayat Khan.

Musharaff was by far the most approachable of the brothers. People invariably felt drawn to his warm, sociable personality. In his contact with mureeds, Musharaff was gentle, compassionate, and humble. His power came from friendliness.

The cultivation of the heart was at the core of Musharaff Khan's teachings. He described this cultivation as a process of evolving love:

"The most important thing in the Sufi teaching is the cultivation of the heart. By cultivating the heart one produces the love-element, which is our inheritance from the Divine Being... By the expansion of that love, the human soul is evolving higher and higher into its full realization of the Oneness of God." [4]

---

3 Sophia Saintsbury-Green, *The Wings of the World or The Sufi Message as I See It* (Deventer, Holland and London: A.E. Kluwer and Luzac & Co., n.d.), p. 29.
4 Pir-o-Murshid Musharaff Khan, *Address VI, The Spirit of Sufism*, Göteborg, 12 October 1956.

Musharaff Khan was constant in his practices, and urged mureeds likewise to be regular in their exercises. He regarded the Sufi prayers, breathing practices, *wazifa*, and zikar, as supreme methods to cleanse the heart of the pain of the past and make it an instrument of divine love. Musharaff Khan was also very open in practicing the Islamic rites of prayer and fasting.

In 1967, at the age of seventy-two, Pir-o-Murshid Musharaff Khan died as a result of a reaction to a vaccine taken in preparation for a planned visit to India. He was buried near the graves of Maheboob Khan and Ali Khan at the cemetery in The Hague called *Oud Eijk en Duinen*. Shortly before his passing, Musharaff said, "Life is a gift of God and death is a gift of God."

Musharaff Khan was a transitional leader. He was the youngest brother of Murshid and the last Indian-born leader of the Sufi Movement. His death marked the end the era of the Brothers. At the same time, his example laid a path for the next generation to follow.

The Four Murshidas

Among the greatest Sufis of early times was Rabi'a al-Adawiyya', whose saintly life served as an inspiration to all who came after her. In later centuries, however, Sufi women generally remained hidden behind veils of social convention that prevented them from fully taking part in the transmission of mystical traditions. Hazrat Inayat Khan saw that this must change. He said, "I see as clear as daylight that the hour is coming when woman will lead humanity to a higher evolution."[1]

Murshid gave the eleventh initiation in his Order, the initiation to the degree of Murshid, to only four mureeds, all four of whom were women: Rabia Ada Martin, Sharifa Lucy Goodenough, Sophia Saintsbury-Green, and Fazal Mai Petronella Egeling. These four women became leading lights of the Order, in Murshid's lifetime and in the years afterward.

Murshida Rabia

Ada Martin was born in San Francisco in 1871. Her parents were pioneering Jewish émigrés from Russia. At the age of nineteen she married, and the following year had a daughter. Ada Martin's life proceeded happily for a time, but then a

1 *The Biography of Pir-o-Murshid Inayat Khan*, p. 243.

sorrow fell over her, and for four years she struggled to find peace and meaning. This was the beginning of her spiritual quest.

She writes: "After certain realizations came in the secret place of my heart, I gave all to Allah and studied, served, and prayed ever to realize His laws, love, mercy, and justice. I made an independent study of comparative religions, and prayed Allah to lead me to the source—thus far it was only drinking from a brook instead of the Ocean of Reality. Then Allah sent my blessed Murshid, spiritually, and later in form."[2]

In 1911 Ada Martin attended a lecture by Inayat Khan at the Vedanta Society in San Francisco. She knew at once that she had met the teacher whom she had long sought. She wrote to him the next day, and he responded, expressing his regret that he was due to leave imminently for Seattle. A luminous vision that night showed him that Mrs. Martin was destined to be his first mureed. She undertook the long journey to Seattle, and there received initiation and the Sufi name Rabia.

In the months and years that followed, Murshid trained Rabia by means of instructions dispatched by post amidst his travels in America and Europe. He addressed her affectionately as *Amma* (Mother), urged her to see Allah in everything, and instructed her in a succession of mystical exercises. In response to her reports, he expressed great satisfaction with her progress and appointed her as his representative in America. When the Sufi Order was established in London, he had Rabia's portrait hung on the wall in the khankah. Murshida Martin later established her own khankah in rural Fairfax, California. In 1923 and 1926, she hosted Murshid during visits to the United States.

After Murshid's death, Murshida Rabia continued her spiritual work, but now apart from the Sufi Movement

2 Ibid, p. 520 (abridged).

based in Geneva. She passed away in San Francisco in 1947. Amongst her papers were found a series of teachings entitled *Gita Dhyana*, and a *Book of Instructions for the Murshid.*

Murshida Sharifa

Born in London in 1876, Lucy Marian Goodenough was the daughter of Colonel W.H. Goodenough (later Lt. General, K.C.B.) and his wife, an Austrian countess. In her youth she traveled widely, mastered several languages, delved deeply into Dante's *Divina Commedia*, and was, for a time, a "leader of fashion" in Vienna.

On meeting Murshid her life changed completely, and she devoted herself entirely to his work, becoming, as Murshid later said, "a foundation stone for the building of the Order." She advanced rapidly on the path and served faithfully as Murshid's scribe, compiling three books based on his teachings: *The Phenomenon of the Soul*; *Love, Human and Divine*; and *Akibat, Life after Death*. In time, she received the successive appointments of *khalifa*, murshida, and *madar-ul-maham silsila sufian*. In the latter capacity she oversaw the Esoteric School and assembled the papers known as the *Gathas*, *Githas*, *Sangathas*, and *Sangithas*.

While some were disconcerted by Murshida Sharifa's austere and reserved manner, Murshid esteemed her a rare soul. He wrote, "Miss Goodenough has proved by her career, firmness and self-sacrifice for the cause to which she has devoted her life… Though retiring, exclusive, and remote by nature, and independent and indifferent in appearance, which has turned many against her and caused many troubles, she has many pearl-like qualities hidden under a hard shell."

The news of Murshid's death severely shook Murshida Sharifa, and she suffered a period of illness. When she reemerged, her personality was transformed. No longer solitary and withdrawn, she became radiant, hospitable, and outgoing. Succeeding Baroness d'Eichtal, she became the national representative of France and attracted a circle of serious students. She gave lectures in Paris and Vienna, and convened classes in Suresnes. A selection of her French lectures were collected in the volume *Soufisme d'Occident*.

Murshida Sharifa died in Suresnes in 1937, depleted in health and wealth, but with a treasure laid up in heaven.

Murshida Sophia

Sophia Saintsbury-Green hailed from an old English family. Raised in a cultured house, from childhood she showed signs of prodigious intellectual curiosity and literary flair. She quenched her scholarly thirst at the wells of ancient wisdom.

As an adult, Sophia Saintsbury-Green was drawn to Theosophy and became a special pupil of Annie Besant. Meeting Murshid, she found in him the personification of all that she sought. She became a mureed, then a khalifa, and finally a murshida. Murshid said of her, "The inspiration and efficiency she has shown in presenting the Message to her people, her sagely character, with her receptivity to the Message, has been of great importance to the cause."

Murshida Saintsbury-Green collaborated with Murshid in creating the Universal Worship, and was ordained the first *cheraga* in 1921. In addition, she poured her energy into publications, editing the journal *Sufism*, and authoring the booklets *The Path to God* and *Human Personality*, and the books *The Wings of the World* and *Memories of Hazrat Inayat Khan*.

A friend who knew her well wrote glowingly of Murshida Saintsbury-Green's qualities: "Exquisite sensitiveness and refinement together with stoic courage; a habit of bearing misrepresentation and detraction silently; lightning quickness of perception and insight into human nature, and utter forgetfulness of self."

Murshida Saintsbury-Green endured poor health for many years. She passed away in 1939.

Murshida Fazal Mai

Petronella Egeling was born in the Netherlands in 1861. She was raised in an orthodox Christian environment, but later turned to Theosophy. She was married for a time. When her husband died, she left the Netherlands to live with friends in Switzerland.

In Lausanne, Petronella Egeling attended a lecture by Murshid and perceived in a flash that it was her life's destiny to serve him and his work. Murshid and his family had recently left London and were living in temporary lodgings in France. Murshid saw that Ms. Egeling was alone in the world and wished to be near him and to be of service to his cause. He therefore accepted her offer to acquire a house in the outskirts of Paris, where she might live with him and his family. A stately house was found in Suresnes, which became Murshid's home and khanqah. Murshid named Petronella Egeling "Fazal Mai" (Blessed Mother) and named the house *Fazal Manzil* (Blessed House).

In the years that followed, a summer school was held annually in the garden of Fazal Manzil. In 1922 Fazal Mai became a *cheraga*, and several months later, a *seraja*, in the Universal Worship. Henceforth she conducted a weekly Sunday service at Fazal Manzil. The following year she became a *shefayat*, and later a *kefayat*, in the Healing Activity. In addition to the Sunday service, she now conducted a weekly healing service. She wrote, "These two services in their simplicity and at the same time in their deep meaning, have become most precious to my heart. To me, as a whole, they are a meditation, an upliftment, a revelation to a greater consciousness, to a higher state of being."[3]

On Christmas morning, 1923, Murshid initiated Fazal Mai as a murshida. From that day onward she made it her daily practice to bless with *fazal* the mureeds of all countries, sending prayerful thoughts to India, to America, and to the various European countries where the Sufi Message had spread, ending with Fazal Manzil.

She wrote, "I look at them all as to my children, sending them my loving thoughts, being happy when they are happy, praying for them in their illnesses and troubles."[4]

Murshida Fazal Mai passed away at Arnhem, the Netherlands, in 1939, just as war was breaking out in Europe. With her death a golden era came to an end.

---

3 *Biography of Pir-o-Murshid Inayat Khan*, p. 499.
4 Ibid, p. 500.

Noor-un-Nisa
by Shrabani Basu

Pirzadi Noor-un-Nisa Inayat Khan was born to Pirani Ameena Begum and Hazrat Inayat Khan in Moscow, in the Vusoko Petrovsky monastery, a short distance from the Kremlin, on 1 January, 1914. Her name meant "light of womanhood." Her title was *pirzadi,* daughter of the pir. At home she was affectionately called Babuli.

As the First World War engulfed Europe, the family left for England, where they lived for the next six years. In London, three more children were born. Noor, only a child herself, mothered all of them.

When Noor was six, the family set sail for France again and began to live in a large house on the outskirts of Paris. Hazrat Inayat Khan called the house Fazal Manzil, and such a place it was. It became an idyllic home for the family, an open house full of music and meditation, with Sufis visiting round the year.

The children played in the garden and loved sitting on the high steps outside the house, looking out over the lights of Paris. They would dress up in their Indian clothes and give concerts before the Sufi guests. The four brothers and sisters formed a quartet.

But in 1927, Hazrat Inayat Khan decided to return to India. He had not been keeping well lately and yearned to go back to his motherland. A few months later they received the devastating news of his death. Ameena Begum went into seclusion. Noor, at the tender age of thirteen, took responsibility for the family and became a mother to her siblings. She began to write poems and short stories, and found solace in these when the burden of domestic chores became too much to bear.

After her schooling, Noor studied child psychology at the Sorbonne and also joined the École Normale to study music. Meanwhile, she was finding her feet as a writer of children's stories. Her stories were published in the Sunday section of *Le Figaro*, and in 1939 her first book, *Twenty Jataka Tales*, was published in England.

However, war clouds were gathering in Europe, and all dreams for the budding writer were quashed as England and France announced war against Germany. In 1940, with the German army ready to enter Paris, Noor and her brother Vilayat took a crucial decision that was to change their lives. Though they were Sufis and believed in nonviolence, they resolved to go to England and volunteer for the war effort.

In a bombed-out London, Vilayat volunteered for the Royal Air Force, and Noor volunteered for the Women's Auxiliary Air Force. There she was trained as a radio operator, joining the first batch of women to train in this field.

But while Noor was tapping away at her Morse code, she was being watched by the Special Operation Executive, who were looking out for people with language skills. The SOE was a crack organization set up by Churchill to aid the resistance movements in occupied countries. Their job was sabotage, and providing arms and money to the resistance.

Noor was called for an interview at the offices of the SOE. She was told that she would be sent as an agent to occupied France after training. She would have no protection, as she would not be in uniform, and she would be shot if she was caught. Without a moment's hesitation, she said she would take the job.

She was now to be trained as a secret agent. It was classic spy school; she was taught to handle guns and explosives, to break locks, to kill silently in the dark, to find sources, to use dead letter boxes and live letter boxes, to practice sending letters in code, and to improve her Morse code. Noor's code name was Madeleine.

Finally the orders for her departure arrived. Armed only with a false passport, some French francs, her pistol and a set of four pills, including the lethal cyanide pill, Noor prepared for her dangerous mission. On the moonlit night of June 16, she was flown covertly across the Channel. Back on French soil, she made her way alone to Paris and joined the circuit. It was the biggest SOE circuit in Europe, called Prosper. Soon Noor settled down and began transmission.

Within a week, disaster struck the Prosper circuit. All the top operatives were captured by the Gestapo, and their wireless sets seized. Noor was advised to go into hiding immediately. Together with another SOE agent, she lay low, gathering information about betrayals and further arrests as the secret police closed in. Eventually London contacted her and asked her to return, as it was too dangerous to stay on; but Noor refused, realizing that she was the last radio link left between London and Paris.

By mid-August Noor was the only British agent in Paris. Single-handedly she now started doing the work of six radio operators. The next three months, Noor was to survive in a dangerous cat and mouse game played by the Gestapo.

Sticking to the rules of her training, she frequently changed her position, kept her transmissions short, and even changed her appearance by constantly dyeing her hair. Noor's communications helped London to pinpoint locations for arms drops, supply money and arms to the French

resistance and organize safe passages home for injured air-
men. The Nazis knew about her and could even hear her
transmissions, but they could not catch her.

In London, her colleagues and seniors were stunned at
her efficiency. Where most radio operators survived for six
weeks, Noor had worked clandestinely for three months. Her
messages were flawless, and her code master felt a special
sense of pride in her.

But the noose was tightening around Noor. Around the
middle of October, she was still safe and would have managed
to catch a flight out of France if she had not been betrayed.
Noor's address was sold to the Nazis for 100,000 francs. With
this information the Gestapo arrested her and took her to
their headquarters at 84 Avenue Foch. Noor immediately
made an escape attempt, but was caught. A few weeks later
she made another daring escape attempt with two other pris-
oners, loosening the sky window and clambering on the roof.
If this escape had succeeded it would have gone down as one
of the most daring escapes of the Second World War.

Noor was now labeled a "highly dangerous" prisoner, and
became the first woman agent to be sent to a German prison.
She was sent to Pforzheim prison on the edge of the Black
Forest, where she stayed for a period of ten months.

Noor was kept in isolation, shackled in chains and foot
irons. She could not feed or clean herself. She was regularly
beaten, tortured and interrogated, but she revealed nothing
about her circuit and gave out no names.

On the night of September 11, Noor was ordered to come
out of her cell. She was driven, handcuffed, to Karlsruhe and
met three of her colleagues there. Together the women were
driven to the railway station and made to board a train.

They reached Dachau at midnight and were led to the
concentration camp. It was to be a long night for Noor. All
night long, she was kicked and beaten; and when her frail
body had slumped on the floor, she was asked to kneel and

was shot point blank at the back of the head by an SS guard. Her last word was "*Liberté.*"

Back in England, both her mother and brother had the same dream. Noor came to them surrounded by blue light. She told them she was free.

On 16 January, 1946, the French awarded Noor the *Croix de Guerre*, the highest civilian honour. Three years later in 1949, England awarded her the George Cross.

More than sixty-five years after the war, Noor's story needs to be preserved for a new generation who need to know about the sacrifices made for freedom. Noor's last word, "Liberté," has been carved on a memorial in Gordon Square to remind the world that a beautiful young woman unhesitatingly sacrificed her life so the world could be free of fascism.

Pir Vilayat

Pirzade Vilayat Inayat Khan was born to Pirani Ameena Begum and Hazrat Inayat Khan in London on June 19th, 1916. From the age of six he was raised at Fazal Manzil in Suresnes, together with his elder sister, Pirzadi Noor-un-Nisa, and younger siblings, Murshidzade Hidayat and Murshidzadi Khair-un-Nisa.

Life in Suresnes revolved around the riveting figure of Hazrat Inayat Khan. But in 1926, Murshid grew abstracted, and the family was seized with foreboding. On one occasion, Murshid gestured toward his shoes, telling his son, "You must follow in my footsteps." Murshid left in September of that year. When the news came from India that Murshid had died, Ameena Begum was devastated, and never fully recovered.

Following their mother's advice, Noor, Vilayat, Hidayat, and Khair-un-Nisa (now known as Claire) studied music at the École Normale de Musique in Paris. Vilayat studied the cello with Maurice Eisenberg. In the summer, lessons were held in San Vicente, Spain, where Vilayat had the privilege of listening to Pablo Casals practice at his seaside villa.

At the age of eighteen, reminded by Murshida Fazal Mai of his mandate from his father, Vilayat resolved to study

philosophy. Commuting between Paris and Oxford, he studied Sufism with Louis Massignon and attended H.H. Price's
lectures on psychology.

In 1940 Europe was again at war. Ameena Begum, Noor,
Vilayat, and Claire removed themselves to England. Ameena
Begum and Claire served as nurses. Noor joined the WAAF
and was recruited to the SOE, with heroic and tragic con-
sequences. Vilayat joined the Royal Air Force and then the
Royal Navy. As a minesweeping officer, Vilayat (then known
by the *nom de guerre* Victor) served on a flotilla of motor
launches that swept channels for Allied landings on the
coasts of France, Belgium, Holland, and Norway. These
operations took place under heavy fire. Once Vilayat's boat
was capsized, and he only narrowly survived.

Vilayat was heartbroken to discover the fate of his sister
Noor, who was his dearest friend. In preparation for his future mission, Shaikh al-Mashaik Maheboob Khan wished to
involve him in the work of the Sufi Movement, but Vilayat's
grief made him demur. He found solace in listening, every
evening, to the whole of the B Minor Mass of Bach on 78
rpm records.

Though desirous to resume his academic studies, as his
mother was unwell and money was in short supply, he took
employment at the India High Commissioner's office in
London, and later at the Pakistani Embassy, where he served
for a time as private secretary to Ghulam Mohammed, the
finance minister of Pakistan.

In 1949 Ameena Begum died, plunging Vilayat again into
sadness. Meanwhile, his career was taking a new turn. He
became a reporter for the Karachi-based newspaper *Dawn*,
and was assigned to report on the Algerian independence
movement. His articles exposing atrocities by the colonial
regime drew the ire of the French government and made
him, for a time, *persona non grata* in France.

Vilayat at last felt that the time had come to dedicate himself to his father's legacy. He undertook contemplative retreats in such varied places as Montserrat, Mt. Athos, Jerusalem, Shiraz, Ajmer, and Gangotri. In Hyderabad, Sayyid Fakhr ad-Din Jili-Kalimi guided him in the methods of the Chishti-Nizami-Kalimi lineage. On his emergence from a forty-day retreat, Pir Fakhr ad-Din ordained him pir, an appointment that was afterward confirmed in Ajmer by Diwan Saulat Husain Chishti.

As the Sufi Movement had meanwhile taken its course without him, Pir Vilayat perceived the untimeliness of asserting his claim to succeed his father, and commenced his own organization, built on the foundation of Murshid's original London constitution for the Sufi Order.

In the succeeding years, Pir Vilayat traveled and lectured extensively, expanding the Order and establishing Sufi centers in several countries. In 1968 he met Murshid Samuel Lewis, who affiliated his circle with Pir Vilayat's organization. The seventies were a time of spiritual and social experimentation, and the Sufi Order drew many young people from the counterculture. Pir Vilayat appreciated idealism of the age, but was wary of its unbalanced excesses.

In 1975 the Order bought a complex of buildings in New Lebanon, New York, built in the eighteenth century by the Shakers. On this site, the Abode of the Message was established. Pir Vilayat took up part-time residence there, along with some seventy-five Sufi initiates and their children. In addition to Sufi activities, the Abode hosted a farm, a bakery, and a school.

Pir Vilayat led a life of constant travel, punctuated by solitary and group retreats. He kept a cave in Chamonix, where the local people knew him as *Le Vieux de la Montagne* (the Old Man of the Mountain). Once, during a retreat, his cave was buried in snow, and angels visited him.

It was Pir Vilayat's contention that meditation was a science and, as such, it must continually advance. His own methodology, while grounded in the Sufi tradition of his father, was informed by Buddhism, yoga, and alchemy, and reinforced with insights from physics and biology.

In the course of his long life, Pir Vilayat initiated thousands of mureeds and spread his father's Sufi Message far and wide. Despite many hardships, he radiated joy to the last. On June 17, 2004, he died in the Oriental Room of Fazal Manzil.

On hearing of Pir Vilayat's passing, His Holiness the Dalai Lama wrote, "I have much admiration for him. His passing is a great loss, especially for those who not only follow the spiritual path, but also believe in tolerance for other religious traditions."[1]

---

1 Letter dated 15 October 2004.

Sufi Ahmed Murad Chishti
by Murshid Wali Ali Meyer

Samuel L. Lewis, later known as Sufi Ahmed Murad Chishti or Murshid Sam, was born in San Francisco, California, on October 18, 1896, to a well-to-do Jewish family. An unusual child, a prodigy, he was reading before the age of three, had completed reading the Old Testament by the time he was six, and reported studying about psychic research at thirteen. His mother claimed to have had a dream of the prophet Samuel before his birth.

The atmosphere of his family home, however, was unusually stiff and repressed. Despite his excellent grades, his father never supported Samuel to go to college because he wasn't interested in money and business. In the later years of his life, when hundreds of young seekers were drawn to him as a spiritual guide, he often told them that it was his own family rejection that made him naturally sympathetic to the younger generation, who were taking a direction not approved by their families.

In November, 1919, while walking on Sutter Street, Samuel saw a display of books in a storefront. He was drawn upstairs and found himself face to face with a little dark-haired Jewish lady. "You can explain the Kabbala?" he asked. "Yes, and all religions." "What is Sufism?" "Sufism is the essence of all religions. It has been brought to the West by Hazrat Inayat Khan." This event marked the beginning of his Sufi studies. The woman was Rabia Martin, Hazrat Inayat Khan's first appointed Murshida.

In June of 1923, before he met Hazrat Inayat Khan, Samuel had a vision of him arriving. Samuel experienced a mystic mergence with him. This inner experience was followed the next day by a summons to meet the pir-o-murshid and receive initiation. It was noon on the summer solstice when he entered the room, and he was frozen into stillness by a tremendous light he saw there. "Come, don't be afraid," a voice said from within that light. Years later, he wrote, "Inasmuch as one met Hazrat Inayat Khan in the world of universal spirit before one met him in the flesh, it established a relationship in the eternity."

In 1925, Samuel took retreat on land at Kaaba Allah in Fairfax, California, owned by Murshida Martin and dedicated to the Sufi work. In the midst of his spiritual practices he sensed what he felt sure was the presence of the legendary Khwaja Khizr. The presence returned the next day and offered Sam the gift of music or poetry. He chose poetry. This encounter motivated Sam to write incessantly, producing a vast body of inspired writing over the next forty-five years.

At the end of ten days, at the hour of the equinox on March 21, Shiva, Buddha, Zoroaster, Moses, and Jesus appeared in vision, and Muhammad on horseback as the Seal of the Prophets. The prophets danced and became one, and, as they danced, Elijah presented Samuel with a robe.

In 1926 he once again met Pir-o-Murshid Inayat Khan, this time at the Beverly Hills Hotel. In the course of six interviews, Hazrat Inayat Khan accepted Samuel's report on his retreat experience, outlined his vision for the Order, encouraged him in his work, and charged him to serve as a "Protector of the Message." Samuel Lewis often testified that this powerful transmission of love-magnetism-*baraka* from his teacher became the strength of his whole life. It transformed him from a very cautious and introverted person into an example of courageous, energetic engagement in life and masterful accomplishment.

From the death of his murshid in 1927 to 1949, Samuel lived alternately in San Francisco and at the Sufi khankah in Fairfax, where he served as the khalif of Murshida Martin, supervisor of spiritual studies of the students, and director of the center in her absence. In 1930 he reported that Hazrat Inayat Khan appeared in vision and pressured open his crown center, and from that time forward Samuel had a living channel of guidance from him, and this poured into his writing of commentaries on his teacher's work.

In 1945 Samuel Lewis was awarded a citation for his work with Army Intelligence (G2) during World War II as a researcher and historian. His exact work was never revealed, but it included reporting troop movements in North Africa, seen clairvoyantly.

In the late 1950s and early 1960s, Samuel Lewis made several trips to the Orient. In India he established relationships with President Radhakrishnan, Swami Ranganathananda Maharaj, Pir-o-Murshid Hasan Sani Nizami, Papa Ram Das and Mother Krishnabai. In Pakistan, Sufi Barkat 'Ali presented him with a robe of transmission.

Samuel Lewis' role as teacher of Sufism was now hastened toward flowering. He began to initiate disciples. Soon young seekers began to flock to his classes. This phenomenon occurred after he had a visitation of the Voice of God while flat on his back in a hospital in 1967.

In 1968, during a visit from Pir Vilayat, Murshid Sam conceived the Dances of Universal Peace. They began with Arabic *hadra* dances and dances using the *Ram Nam* mantra. After that, the heavens opened, and he began to receive dances, often in visions interrupting his dreams. Sacred phrases and prayers from many of the world's sacred traditions were now manifesting, along with music and expressive movements.

Murshid Sam saw that the dances would go all over the world because they belonged to God and were an answer to the cry of humanity. He said his plan for world peace was simple: get people to eat, dance, and pray together. From their humble beginning, the Dances of Universal Peace are now flourishing in more than thirty countries. Pir Vilayat requested Murshid Sam to form a separate corporate entity. That entity, the Sufi Ruhaniat International, now represents his spiritual transmission.

Murshid Samuel Lewis often said that all the credit for everything he accomplished in his life should go to Hazrat Inayat Khan. On January 15, 1971, he died after a concussion suffered in a fall. His tomb is at Lama Foundation in New Mexico, where it has become a place for retreat and pilgrimage. A *hadith* of the Prophet Muhammad was chosen by Samuel Lewis as his epitaph. It reads, "On that day the Sun shall rise in the West and all men seeing will believe."

THE INNER SCHOOL

The Sufi Order

The Sufi Order is the same school which has existed in different parts of the East as an esoteric school and which, during the period of Islam, was accepted and carried out by the rationalistic philosophers of Islam. The tradition of this Order is traced from the time of Abraham, and the genealogy of the murshids of this Order can be found from the time of the Prophet Muhammad. The later development of the Sufi Order, which is called Chishtiyya, culminated in the present Order of Sufis, which is established in the West in order that through the medium of the ancient wisdom, East and West should be united beyond the boundaries of differences and thus unite to the best advantage of humanity at large.

The Objects of the Order

1. To realize and spread the knowledge of unity, the religion of love and wisdom, so that the bias of faiths and beliefs may of itself fall away, the human heart may overflow with love, and all hatred caused by distinctions and differences may be rooted out.

2. To discover the light and power latent in man, the secret of all religion, the power of mysticism, and the essence of philosophy, without interfering with customs or beliefs.

83

3. To help to bring the world's two opposite poles, East and West, close together by the interchange of thoughts and ideals, that the universal brotherhood may form of itself, and man may meet with man beyond the narrow national and racial boundaries.[1]

---

1 Constitution of the Sufi Order, Geneva (n.d.).

The Symbol of the Order
by Hazrat Inayat Khan

The symbol of the Sufi Order, which is a heart with wings, is symbolic of its ideal. The heart is both earthly and heavenly. The heart is a receptacle on earth of the divine spirit and, when it holds the divine spirit, it soars heavenward; the wings picture its rising. The crescent in the heart symbolizes responsiveness; it is the heart that responds to the spirit of God that rises. The crescent is a symbol of responsiveness because it grows fuller by responding more and more to the sun as it progresses. The light one sees in the crescent is the light of the sun. It gets more light with increasing response, so it becomes fuller of the light of the sun. The star in the heart of the crescent represents the divine spark reflected in the human heart as love, which helps the crescent toward its fullness.[1]

---

1 *The Sufi Message* (1964), vol. 9, pp. 19–20.

Initiation in the Sufi Order
by Hazrat Inayat Khan

In considering the question of being initiated into the Sufi Order, there is, in the first place, the inclination to know something different from what is taught in the world. One feels the desire to seek for something, though one knows not what. One feels that the opposites, good and evil, right and wrong, friend and foe, are not so far apart as one used to think.

At the same time, the heart is felt to be more sympathetic than ever before, and the sense of justice makes one wish to judge oneself before judging others.

This all shows that one may look for a guide through these unknown paths.

Then there is the feeling, especially after reading or hearing something about Sufism, that one is already really a Sufi, that one is at one with the circle of Sufis. One may now feel drawn to the spirit of the teacher from whose hand initiation may be taken.

And thirdly there is the feeling, after studying the books published by the movement, or after speaking with the pir-o-murshid, that the Message is genuine.

Then the question arises: what is meant by initiation? Initiation, or in Sufi terms *bayat*, first of all has to do with the relationship between the pupil and the murshid. The murshid is understood to be the counselor on the spiritual path. He does not give anything to or teach the pupil, the mureed, for he cannot give what the latter already has; he cannot teach what his soul has always known. What he does in the life of the mureed is to show him how he can clear his path towards the light within by his own self. This is the only purpose of man's life on earth. One may attain the purpose of life without a personal guide, but to try to do so is to be like a ship traversing the ocean without a compass. To take initiation then means entrusting oneself, in regard to spiritual matters, to a spiritual guide.

To become an initiate in the Sufi Order, therefore, implies a willingness to agree with its teachings and objects; a willingness to cease to attach importance to the differences of the world's various faiths, and to see in all the masters only one embodiment of the divine Spirit: and thirdly, it implies that one is not already following another course of spiritual training. In such a case, why go to another kind of teacher as well? It would be like traveling in two boats, one foot in each. When each boat goes its own way, although they meet in the end at the same goal, yet the traveler will sink in the sea. No one could seek guidance under two teachers except out of lack of patience with the one or lack of confidence in the other, making him still cling to the first.

The objects one should have in taking initiation under the murshid are: to realize the self within and without; to know and communicate with God, whom alone the world worships; to kindle the fire of divine love, which alone has any value; to be able the read nature's manuscript and to be able to see into the world unseen; to learn how to control oneself; to light the torch of the soul and to kindle the fire of the heart; to journey through this positive existence and arrive, in this life, at the goal at which every soul is bound in the end to arrive. It is better to arrive in the light than to be only transported through the dark.

Are there any conditions imposed in a would-be initiate? No one need fear taking initiation from the idea that he undertakes something he may not be able to fulfill. If he does not wish to progress beyond a certain point, that is only for himself to say. The only thing that happens when a person is initiated, is that from the hour of initiation one is the brother of all in the Sufi Movement, of all other Sufis outside the Sufi Movement, of all knowers of truth, whether they call themselves Sufi or not, and of every human being, without distinction of caste, creed, race, nation, or religion. One is the companion of the illuminated souls of the Sufis living on earth and of those who have passed to the other side of life. Thus one is linked with the chain of murshids and prophets, and so enabled to receive the light running through this current, through the chain of masters. And one is the confidant to the murshid and of the Order. Therefore the initiate takes a vow in his heart to make use, to the best of his ability, of all he receives from the Sufi teaching and practices, not using any parts for selfish purposes. These teachings have been kept secret for thousands of years, so why should they go out of the Order without the pir-o-murshid's authorization?

One may ask why there is any secrecy about the teaching. If true, why should it not be scattered broadcast? This implies that secrecy is objectionable. The answer, however, is quite easy. A certain secrecy is necessary, in that some of the Sufi conceptions might easily be misunderstood and misused, were they exposed to the general public. The earnest pupil will not speak of them without due consideration of his audience.

A certain medicine may be good for a sick person at a certain time, but this does not mean it should be used by every sick person in the world. Nor would it be any advantage to anyone, if the exact medicine were to be published indiscriminately. It there should arise need to say what it was, the doctor would not withhold the information.

Where there is a need to explain the Sufi teachings, the murshid will explain them. The books published by the Sufi Movement set forth many of the teachings, so that it cannot be said that they are kept rigidly secret. But the very intimate thoughts, to which the Sufi is accustomed, are naturally not uttered indiscriminately, any more than an ordinary person will speak of his private affairs to a stranger.

The fruit must be of a certain degree of ripeness before its taste becomes sweet. So the soul must be of a certain development before it will handle wisdom with wisdom. The developed soul shows his fragrance in his atmosphere, color, the expression of his countenance, and sweetness of his personality, as a flower spreads its fragrance around, and as a fruit, when ripe, changes its color and becomes sweet.[1]

---

1 *The Sufi Message* (1960), vol. 1, pp. 46-51 (abridged).

What is Necessary for a Mureed
by Hazrat Inayat Khan

The first thing most necessary for a mureed is to try to keep up the spiritual exercises which are given, without any break. If you are tired, if you were occupied too much, if conditions were not favorable, I do not mean that it is urged upon you, but I mean that it is for your betterment to keep those exercises without a gap between them. If they are seeds which you sow in the ground, they take root and a plant comes. There are some plants which come quicker, others which take time to bear fruit. But still the spiritual sowing has its result, and a sure result. Never therefore to doubt, to be discouraged, to give up hope; but to continue, persevering in this path.

Now the second necessity for the mureed is the study part. It must not be a study only as the reading of a book: it must be a study of engraving upon one's heart the *Gathas*, *Gathekas*, all the literature that is given, however simple it might seem to grasp it. Because you will find that it is creative in itself. It is a phrase just now; after six months the same phrase will flourish, there will come branches, flowers, and fruits in that phrase. It is a simple phrase, but it is a living phrase. The more you study and grasp it, the more your heart will be creative. Therefore do not consider it a study only, but a meditation, even in your studies.

The third important thing in the life of a mureed is to live a life of balance between activity and repose, of regularity. Not too much work, nor too much rest: a balance between activity and repose. Because when we put the idea before the world we shall be responsible to show it in our lives. Therefore our lives must be as balanced as possible. Besides that, in eating, in drinking, there must be a kind of moderation, which I am sure many of us have. And a kind of consideration from the meditative point of view. Because for the spiritual growth a certain food is more recommended than another. Therefore we in the spiritual path cannot always be neglectful of that question.

And now there comes the fourth question: how must our attitude be towards others? Towards the mureeds our attitude must be affectionate sympathy. Towards non-mureeds our attitude must be tolerant sympathy. The best thing in the world is not to force upon others what we understand and what we believe. By forcing it upon others we only spoil them. By discussing, arguing with them, we do not accomplish anything. So you can quite see that it is the path of silence. The more we keep our lips closed the more the way is open, the more doors are open for us. The attitude itself opens them. Our attitude with others must therefore be humble, unpretentious, and ordinary.

Now the fifth thing. We must not leave our meditation and prayers just to those fixed times when we do, because that is only the winding of the thing. But in our everyday life we ought to bring the sense of it into our action, in everything we do at home or outside. We must use that latent power and inspiration aroused by our meditations; we should make use of it. By practicing to make use of it, we shall benefit ourselves and others by all we are doing.[1]

---

1 *Supplementary Papers,* "Class for Mureeds II" (privately distributed).

The Structure of the Order

The Sufi Order has as its head the Shaikh-ul-Mashaikh, the Pir-o-Murshid, to direct the Order throughout the world.

The Pir-o-Murshid designates his senior representative, Murshid, and junior representative, Khalif. The Pir-o-Murshid makes rules and appoints councils for the work of the Sufi Order. He presides at the Jamiat meetings. Every decision made at the Jamiat is submitted to him for his approval. His successor is designated by him.

The Mashaikh, or Murshid, has the right to appoint Leaders and Conductors for the work of the Order, and to propose candidates to be designated as Khalif. He directs all the activities in his jurisdiction with the assistance of the Khalifs working within his jurisdiction. He has the right to initiate candidates up to the ninth degree.

The Shaikh, or Khalif, has the right to appoint a Conductor, and he proposes a Leader for the working of the Order, to be appointed by the Murshid. He has the right of giving initiations up to the sixth degree.

The Leader in the Sufi Order is the senior assistant of the Khalif, and a Conductor in the Order is the junior assistant.

The Leader in the Sufi Order gives assistance to the Khalif in holding for him the Sacred Reading.

The Conductor in the Order is the second assistant to the Khalif, who assists the Khalif in attending to the group of the candidates prepared for initiation.

Circles of Initiates

There are four Circles of initiates in the Sufi Order:

1. The Study Circle
   First Initiation, Elementary
   Second Initiation, Junior
   Third Initiation, Senior

2. The Advanced Circle
   Fourth Initiation, Associate
   Fifth Initiation, Licentiate
   Sixth Initiation, Initiate

3. The Inner Circle
   Seventh Initiation, Talib
   Eighth Initiation, Mureed
   Ninth Initiation, Sufi

4. The Higher Circle
   Tenth Initiation, Khalif
   Eleventh Initiation, Murshid
   Twelfth Initiation, Pir-o-Murshid

Courses in the Sufi Order

Course for the Conductor in the Order
   Three series of *Gathas*.

Course for the Leader in the Order
   Three series of *Githas*.

Course for the Khalif
  Three series of *Sangathas*.
  He must write a treatise on the *Gathas*.
  He is to speak on any subject of the *Gathas*.

Course for the Murshid
  Three series of *Sangithas*.
  He must write a treatise on the *Githas*.
  He is to speak on any subject of the *Githas*.

Bylaws

Jamiat

The Jamiat of the Sufi Order has two circles:
1. Jamiat Khas, and 2. Jamiat Am. Jamiat Khas consists of the Murshids and Khalifs. The members of the Jamiat Am are elected, or appointed by Pir-o-Murshid.

Jamiat concerns itself with the affairs of the esoteric activities of the Order.

The designation of Murshids and of Khalifs mostly takes place publicly. The ceremony is attended by the initiated members of the Order.

The Khalif receives a *bhagwa* robe and a testimonial.
The Murshid receives a shawl and a testimonial.
The Pir-o-Murshid has a turban of distinction.

There is a Madar-ul-Maham (Minister of the affairs concerning the Sufi Order), who acts as General-Secretary to the Jamiat and keeps in communication with the activities concerning the Order throughout the world. The Madar-ul-Maham is the custodian of the literature of the Esoteric School, and he sends all testimonials given for different initiations. The seal of the Order is entrusted to him.

No other teachings will be given to the candidates of those initiated than those of the Pir-o-Murshid or of the past masters of this particular Order, except interpretations of the Pir-o-Murshid's teachings given by Murshids or explanations of the same given by Khalifs.[1]

---

1 Constitution of the Sufi Order, Geneva (n.d.).

THE PATH

Steps on the Path
by Hazrat Inayat Khan

Sufis have various paths of attainment, for instance, the paths of *salik* and *rind*; and among those who tread the path of salik, of righteousness, there are many whose method of spiritual attainment is devotion. Devotion requires an ideal, and the ideal of the Sufis is the God-ideal. They attain to this ideal by a gradual process. They first take bayat, initiation, from the hand of one whose presence gives them confidence that he will be a worthy counselor in life and a guide on the path as yet untrodden, and who, at the same time, shows them in life the image of the rasul personality, the personality of the ideal man. He is called pir-o-murshid.

There are several steps on the path. This is a vast subject, but condensing it, I would say that there are five principal steps. The first is responsiveness to beauty of all kinds, in music, in poetry, in color or line. The second is one's exaltation by beauty, the feeling of ecstasy. The third step is tolerance and forgiveness. These come naturally without striving for them. The fourth is that one accepts, as if they were a pleasure, the things one dislikes and cannot stand—in the place of a bowl of wine, the bowl of poison. The fifth step is taken when one feels the rein of one's mind in one's hand; for then one begins to feel tranquility and peace at will. This is just like riding on a very vigorous and lively horse, yet holding the reins firmly and making it walk at the speed one desires. When this step is taken, the mureed becomes a master.

The time of initiation is meant to be a time for clearing away all the sins of the past. The cleansing of sins is like a bath in the Ganges. It is the bath of the spirit in the light of knowledge. From this day, the page is turned. The mureed makes his vow to the murshid that he will treasure the teachings of the masters in the past and keep them secret, that he will make good use of the teachings and of the powers gained by them, and that he will try to crush his *nafs*, his ego. He vows that he will respect all the masters of humanity as the one embodiment of the ideal man and will consider himself the brother not only of all the Sufis in the order to which he belongs, but also outside that order of all those who are Sufis in spirit, although they may call themselves differently; and of all mankind, without distinction of caste, creed, race, nation or religion.

Sufis engage in *halqa*, a circle of Sufis sitting and practicing zikar and *fikar* so that the power of the one helps the other. Furthermore, they practice *tawajjuh*, a method of receiving knowledge and power from the teacher in silence. This way is considered by Sufis to be the most essential and desirable.

Sometimes a receptive mureed attains in a moment, greater perfection than he might attain in many years of study or practice; because it is not only his own knowledge and power that the murshid imparts, but sometimes it is the knowledge and power of rasul, and sometimes even of God. It all depends upon the time and upon how the expressive and receptive souls are focused.

The task of the Sufi teacher is not to force a belief on a mureed, but to train him so that he may become illuminated enough to receive revelations himself.[1]

---

1 *The Sufi Message* (1964), vol. 10, pp. 85-6.

Shaikh, Rasul and Allah
by Hazrat Inayat Khan

The friendship with the shaikh has no other motive than guidance in seeking God. As long as your individuality lasts it will last; as long as you are seeking God it will last; as long as guidance is needed it will last. The friendship with the shaikh is called *fana fi'sh-shaikh*, and it merges into the friendship with rasul. When the mureed realizes the existence of the spiritual qualities beyond the earthly being of the murshid, that is the time when he is ready for *fana fi'r-rasul*.

Rasul is the personification of the light of guidance, which a mureed, according to his evolution, idealizes. Whenever the devotee remembers him on the earth, in the air, at the bottom of the sea, he is with him. Devotion to rasul is a stage that cannot be omitted in the attainment of divine love. This stage is called *fana fi'r-rasul*.

After this comes *fana fi'Llah*, when the love of rasul merges in the love of Allah. Rasul is the master who is idealized for his lovable attributes, his kindness, goodness, holiness, mercy. His merits are intelligible. His form is not known, only the name which constitutes his qualities. But Allah is the name given to that ideal of perfection where all limitation ceases, and in Allah the ideal ends.

A person does not lose the friendship with the pir nor with rasul, but he beholds murshid in rasul and rasul in

Allah. Then for guidance, for advice, he looks to Allah alone. From those who see Allah, rasul and shaikh disappear. They see only Allah in the pir and rasul. They see everything as Allah and see nothing else.

A mureed, by devotion to the murshid, learns the manner of love, standing with childlike humility, seeing in the face of every being on earth his pir's blessed image reflected. When rasul is idealized, he sees all that is beautiful reflected in the unseen ideal of rasul. Then he becomes independent, even of merit—which also has an opposite pole, and in reality does not exist, for it is comparison that makes one thing appear better than the other—and he loves only Allah, the perfect ideal, who is free from all comparison, beyond this ideal.

Then he himself becomes love, and the work of love has been accomplished. Then the lover himself becomes the source of love, the origin of love, and he lives the life of Allah, which is called *baqa bi'Llah*. His personality becomes divine personality. Then his thought is the thought of God, his word the word of God, his action the action of God, and he himself becomes love, lover, and beloved.[1]

---

1 *The Sufi Message* (1962), vol. 5, pp. 186-87 (abridged).

Freeing the Soul
by Hazrat Inayat Khan

The ultimate freedom of the soul is gained by concentration, by contemplation, by meditation and realization. What concentration is needed for the freedom of the soul? The concentration on that object which is prescribed by one's spiritual teacher, that by the thought of that particular object one may be able to forget oneself for a moment. And then what contemplation is necessary? The contemplation that "this, my limited self, is no longer myself but God's own instrument, God's temple, which is made in order that the Name of God be glorified." What meditation is required? The meditation on the thought of God, the Being of God, forgetting absolutely one's limited self. And the realization is this, that then whatever voice comes to one is God's voice, every guidance is God's guidance, every impulse is divine impulse, every action is done by God. It is in this way that the soul is made free, and in the freedom of the soul lies the purpose of life.[1]

---

1 *The Sufi Message* (1962), vol. 7, p. 197.

Knowing God
by Hazrat Inayat Khan

Idealizing

Every sincere and earnest believer in God experiences this stage. It is the stage in which he stands before God in humility and gentleness, or with repentance for his sins and for his faults. He understands that he is a mere drop in relation to the ocean, that he is most limited compared to a most unlimited God, that he is most feeble while the other is Almighty. He realizes that there is a Being filled with all the virtues and goodness and justice and mercy and compassion imaginable. Whatever be his religion, everyone experiences this first stage, being a faithful believer in God.

This is the ideal taught from childhood on, even in ancient times. Today, some teach it, and some do not. Education has taken a different turn, with the result that idealizing God has been disappearing from the stage of life.

Recognizing

Recognizing is the second step. At this stage the believer in God thinks of Him not only as in heaven, where all praise, worship, honor, and respect are due to Him, but recognizes that He is on earth also.

104

If we study carefully, we come to see that as God is the Creator, He must have something to create from. If He created out of something already made, then that substance must have been made by some other god, or perhaps a thousand gods—and even then we may not have come to the end! But this cannot be. The whole Creation is from one Being whose wisdom, art, and power are unlimited. He creates of Himself, with His own power. Therefore the Creation and the Creator are not two, just as man and his body are not two. They are two, but at the same time they are not. If you recognize God, you can recognize Him not only in heaven, but on earth also. Those who recognize Him, see Him in all.

Communicating with God   *Communion*

Once you begin to recognize God in man, you do not see man anymore, but God. The man is the surface, while the God is deep in him. Such recognition brings you in touch with everyone's inmost being, and you know more about them than they know themselves. The seer sees God with his own eyes, and also recognizes his divine Beloved in every form, in every name. He reaches Him and touches the God part in every being, however limited that individual appears to be on the surface. From now on there comes a softness in his nature, a magnetism, a charm, a beauty in him rarely to be found. Those people who have attained to this stage are able to meet people with awakened minds. The lover is always very careful when he is with his Beloved. He becomes thoughtful and tender. Now there remain only two more steps.

Realization

It is after feeling the presence of God and after being in communication with Him that we come to realize Him. When you can touch God in everybody, then God tells you about Himself, because He sees you have no hate, no prejudice. You have seen your Beloved, and your Beloved tells you all. Realization is still difficult, for it involves discerning the difference between "I" and "you." What is the difference? It is a great question. The "I" and "you" only remain as long as we see ourselves. But when we rise above or beyond them, thought brings us nearer and nearer to God in that consciousness in which we all unite. Self-realization is where the word is silent. The sage cannot say more than this because the subject is so vast. When we come to this conception, we find it is altogether too subtle, too vast to express.

Perfection

Perfection and annihilation is that stage at which there is no longer "I" and no longer "you," where there is what there is.[1]

---

1 *The Sufi Message* (1967), vol. 12, pp. 68-75 (abridged).

Dying Before Death
by Hazrat Inayat Khan

Sufism is learned chiefly in order that a person may know what will happen to him after death, in that being which is our real being, though usually it is hidden from us.

After the physical death, the life that cannot die bears man up, and he remains always alive. Both on earth and on the sea, we living beings exist, having both elements in our form, the earth and the water. The beings of the sea are formed of earth as well. We have water also in our constitution. Yet the sea is as strange to us as the earth is to the creatures of the sea. Neither would like their place exchanged; and if it so happens that they are out of their element, it leads them to their end. It is because the fish has not realized that it is also an earthly being and that the earth is its element too, that it cannot live on earth; and in the same way, beings on land, whose life depends on getting to shore, fail when they believe that they will sink in the sea.

If we were dropped into the sea, it would be a terrible thing. We would be convinced that we would go to the bottom, that we would be drowned. It is our fear that makes us go to the bottom, and our thought; except for this, there is no reason why we should sink. The sea lifts up the whole ship in which a thousand people are traveling and in which tons of weight are loaded; why should it not lift up our little body?

Our inner being is like the sea, our external being as the earth. So it is with the word called death. It is the sea part of ourselves, where we are taken from our earth part, and, not being accustomed to it, we find the journey unfamiliar and uncomfortable, and call it death. To the seaman the sea is as easy to journey upon, whenever he chooses to, as the land. Christ, in connection with this subject, said to Peter, "O thou of little faith, wherefore didst thou doubt?"[1] Both in Sanskrit and Prakrit, liberation is called *taran*, which means swimming. It is the power to swim which makes water the abode of the earthly fish, and for those who swim in the ocean of eternal life, in the presence as well as in the absence of the body, it becomes their everlasting abode.

The swimmer plays with the sea. At first he swims a little way, then he swims far out. Then he masters it, and at last it is his home, his element, as the earth is. He who has mastered these two elements has gained all mastery.

The divers in the port of Ceylon, and the Arabs on the Red Sea, dive down into the sea. First they stop up their ears, eyes, lips, and their nose, then they dive and bring up pearls. The mystic also dives in to the sea of consciousness by closing his senses from the external world and thus entering into the abstract plane.

The work of the Sufi is to take away the fear of death. This path is trodden in order to know in life what will be with us after death. As it is said in the Hadith, "*Mutu qabla an tamutu*" or "Die before death." To take off this mortal garb, to teach the soul that it is not this mortal, but is that immortal being, so that we may escape the great disappointment which death brings, this is what is accomplished in life by a Sufi.[2]

---

1 Matthew 14:31.
2 *The Sufi Message* (1962), vol. 5, pp. 45-47.

The Light of God
by Nargis Dowland

The light that is guiding the traveler upon the spiritual path is, in reality, the light that is shining from his own soul; when his inner eyes are opened he will always see this light before him lighting the path he is treading; and everyone he meets, and everything, animate or inanimate, becomes illuminated before his view. At first this truth is not understood by the disciple; he sees a light, and because he sees, he follows until he becomes bewildered by seeing it in so many places, which before to him were but darkness. This leads him into strange paths, and many truths are thus revealed to him, for everything upon which this light falls reveals its secret to the seer. But the disciple has not realized the mystery of the Light of Guidance until he has ceased to follow it outside himself. There comes a time in the spiritual development when the traveler to the goal closes his eyes; the meaning of this is that he seeks nothing, not even the Light of Guidance, outside himself. When this stage has been reached, he knows that the light, which so long had been before his sight, leading him by so many ways, was a reflection of the Light of God within his own soul, which was turned Godward, and so focused upon the Only Light.[1]

---

1 Nargis (Jessie Eliza Dowland), *Between the Desert and the Sown* (Southampton: The Sufi Movement, n.d.), p. 41.

Finding God
by Nargis Dowland

God is hidden by many veils of illusion in order that He may be found. The only way to find truth is to seek it in the most unlikely places. It is only by drawing away the veils, one by one, by letting go illusion after illusion, even at the cost of our heart's blood, that will finally open the inner eyes by which we can perceive truth; and when the last illusion has gone we find that, after all, God was never hidden, but it was we who were blinded; for all the time He was close beside us, although we could not see Him.[1]

---

1 *Between the Desert and the Sown*, p. 107.

Roadmaking
by Nargis Dowland

What all those who try to live the inner life are really doing is roadmaking. Thousands today are trying to find the path to God; the majority know that somewhere it exists, but cannot find out where it is. Now the work of the roadmaker is to make the road; the only way this road can be made is by treading it; when many feet have trodden a path, it will at last become clear to the view of all. At the present time it is obscure, because only a few, at long intervals, have passed that way; and there has been time after their passing for the way again to become obliterated and overgrown with the thick undergrowth, so that even the entrance remains hidden. Steamrollers and mechanical contrivances cannot be used for making this road, because the way is too narrow, too steep and too winding; it is also very difficult to follow, sometimes passing over chasms, sometimes besides precipices. There is only one thing able to make a highway, and that is willing feet.[1]

---

1 *Between the Desert and the Sown*, pp. 42-43 (abridged).

The Spirit of Guidance
by Nargis Dowland

The body of the Master (if one can use such a term; magnetic field would better express it), is composed of the perfected souls of those beings who, in every age since the beginning of this earth, have reached the stage of evolution known to mystics as perfection; the guiding or informing Spirit is the same in every holy name and form, and collectively they form the embodiment of the One Christ.

As individuals, they have been and still are, separate, distinct, and living; but their souls form One Spirit which is known as the Spirit of Guidance.

This will, in some measure, explain to those who have understanding, the mystery of many masters but only One Master, many religions but only One Religion, many truths but only One Truth; and there is still a further mystery: every soul that reaches perfection is an enrichment of that Mystical Body, which by the evolution of perfected souls, attains its own fulfillment. But of this, words may not be spoken; only to the closed senses can it be revealed.[1]

---

1 *At the Gate of Discipleship* (Southampton: The Sufi Movement, n.d.), pp. 44-45.

METHODS AND PRECEPTS

Practices
by Hazrat Inayat Khan

The entire universe in all its activity has been created through the concentration of Allah. Every being in the world is occupied, consciously or unconsciously, in some act of concentration. Good and evil are alike the result of concentration. The stronger the concentration, the greater the result; lack of concentration is the cause of failure in all things. For this world and the other, for material as well as spiritual progress, concentration is most essential.

The power of will is much greater than the power of action, but action is the final necessity for the fulfillment of will. There are seven kinds of concentration in Sufism:

1. *Namaz*—for control of the body.
2. *Wazifa*—for control of the thought.
3. *Zikar*—for physical purification.
4. *Fikar*—for mental purification.
5. *Qasab*—for entering into the spirit.
6. *Shaghal*—for entering into the abstract.
7. *'Amal*—for complete annihilation.

Perfection is reached by the regular practice of these concentrations, passing through three grades of development:

Fana fi'sh-shaikh—annihilation in the astral plane.
Fana fi'r-rasul—annihilation in the spiritual plane.
Fana fi'Llah—annihilation in the abstract.

After passing through these three grades, the highest state of *baqa bi'Llah* (annihilation in the eternal conscious-ness), which is the destination of all who travel by this path, is attained.

Breath is the first thing to be well studied. This is the very life, and also the chain which connects material existence with the spiritual. Its right control is a ladder leading from the lowest to the highest stage of development. Its science is to be mastered by the favor of the murshid, the guiding light of Allah. [1]

---

1 *A Sufi Message of Spiritual Liberty* (London: The Theosophical Pub-lishing Society, 1914), pp. 55-56.

Postures
by Hazrat Inayat Khan

There are four principal postures. One is used in the zikar and fikar, and that is called the posture of the Cupid. This posture is given to make the heart melted. I do not mean to say that without that posture the zikar does not work upon the person, but at the same time, with that posture it has a greater effect; and that posture is to take the sinew cord of the left leg under the knee, between the two toes of the right foot, and to sit cross-legged. This posture has an influence on the heart, it makes the heart responsive.

And the second posture is a simple cross-legged, sitting simply cross-legged with the two hands on the knees. This helps one to have ease and comfort and inspiration and peace. Then there is a third posture that is to sit on the left heel, and the right heel taken inwardly. This posture is the posture of the adept. The posture before is the posture of the king, because it gives happiness and comfort and pleasure to those who are accustomed to sit cross-legged; but the third is the posture of the adept who gains self-control, and who practices self discipline.

The fourth posture is the posture of the sage, and that posture is to take one foot on one thigh, and the other on the other thigh. It is a most difficult posture, but it is a posture

117

by which perfection is gained. Now you might think: what is the reason? The reason is that as two legs are two currents, going outwardly through the heart, so are two hands; and by putting two feet on the thigh, you have closed two currents; and then, by closing your palms and the thumbs, you close four currents. Then the heart, which is the sun, has no way of sending out, of release, sending out its current. Therefore what does it do? It begins to expand in itself; and therefore, it begins to become large in itself, and more illuminated, and more powerful; and all that is latent in it comes out, and by that, perfection is gained. These four postures, therefore, are the most wonderful postures to be remembered.[1]

---

1 *Sangitha I*, "Ta'lim/Teaching" (privately distributed, abridged).

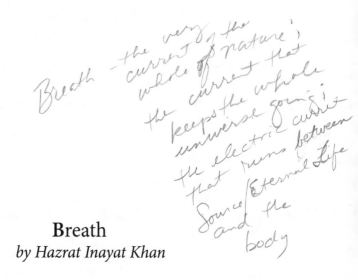

*Breath — the very current of the whole of nature?
the current that keeps the whole universe going;
the electric current that runs between
Source/Eternal Life and the body*

Breath
by Hazrat Inayat Khan

To a mystic, the subject of breath is the deepest of all the subjects with which mysticism or philosophy is concerned, because breath is the most important thing in life. The very life of man is breath. He lives in the presence of breath, and in the absence of breath, man is called a corpse.

Breath is that within ourselves which keeps all the parts of the body in connection with one another, working together, depending upon one another; it is that which enables man to move, to put his muscles into action, to keep the whole mechanism of the body at work. There is no other force or power concerned with all this than the power of breath.

Wherever we look, be it the changes of the seasons, the changes of the weather, or even the constant circles which the earth describes on its journey, all these show the same underlying current, the current of the whole of nature, which is the real breath. The whole universe is going on with a certain rhythm; there is a current which keeps the whole universe going. It is one breath, and yet it is many breaths.[1]

Breath is a channel through which all the expression of the innermost life can be given. Breath is an electric current that runs between the everlasting life and the mortal frame.

1 *The Sufi Message* (1962), vol. 7, pp. 102-4 (abridged).

119

Those who have attained any intuition or miraculous power or any power, have achieved it by the help of the breath. But the first essential thing is a pure channel for the breath, and that channel is the human body. If the channel is blocked, there is not possibility for the breath to flow freely. Breath in itself is pure, but if the channel through which it works is not right, it becomes impure.

The breath makes a circuit through the body, and the channel through which it makes the circuit is the spine. The mystics give this channel great importance; they call it the serpent. They picture it as a serpent holding its tail in its mouth. In almost all symbols the serpent represents the channel of the breath. When this channel is made clear by the method of breathing, then this is not only a help to the physical health, but it also opens up the faculties of intuition and the doors that are within, where lies the real happiness of man. In order to clear this channel of all that blocks the way, one must follow the rules of mystical ablutions and of rhythmic breathing.

People look for phenomena, but there is no better phenomena that breath itself, because breath is life and light; and in the breath is the source of life and light. In the mastery of breath the secret of both worlds is hidden.[2]

---

2 *The Wisdom of Sufism: Sacred Readings from the Gathas* (Shaftesbury, Dorset: Element Books, 2000), pp. 132-33 (abridged).

Subtle Centers
by Hazrat Inayat Khan

As there are different organs of senses, so there are five centers of inner perception. These centers are seats of the intuitive faculties. Two among them are of great importance: the heart and the head. If the Sufi training differs from that of the Yogis, it is in the training of both these centers together, by which the Sufi achieves balance. The head without the heart shows dry intellect. The heart without the head represents an unbalanced condition. Balance is the use of both these faculties. The Sufi training is based upon this principle.

The centers may be likened to the space that one finds in the apple. It is an *akasha*, an accommodation, where not only scent, touch, hearing and sight are perceived, but even the thought and feeling of another; the condition in the atmosphere, the pleasure and displeasure of one's fellow man are perceived, and if the sense of perception is keener, then even past, present and future can be perceived. When man does not perceive in this way, it does not mean that it is foreign to his nature; it only means that the soul has not developed that power of perception in his body. The absence of such fine perception naturally causes depression and confusion, for the soul longs for a keen perception.

The physical body is made of matter, its sustenance is matter; but the centers of perception are of still finer matter, and though they are located in the physical body, no nourishment can reach them except that which is drawn through the breath, the fine substance which is not even visible. In the language of the mystics it is called *nur*, which means light. The body does not only want food, but also breath, in other words, vibration; and that vibration is given to it by the repetition of sacred words. These centers are the akasha, or domes, where every sound has its echo; and the echo once produced in this akasha or *asman* reaches all other asmans which exist within and without. Therefore the repetition of a sacred word has not only to do with oneself and one's life, but it spreads and rises higher than man can imagine, and wider than he can perceive.[1]

The heart is the root of the body, which is its plant. It is the heart which is formed first in the womb of the mother, and all other organs of the body are formed afterwards. Therefore the condition of the whole body depends on the condition of the heart. The exercise of zikar sets the heart to rhythm, which regulates the working of the whole system, its psychic power in this way regulating the higher planes of existence. Certainly, the heart of flesh is not the heart which is the depth of man's being. But the heart of flesh, being directly in focus to the inner or real heart, reflects in its turn that which happens to be in the inner heart. It is, therefore, that this piece of flesh is called "heart," it being the only factor which represents the heart within.[2]

There is a center which is the most important; it is the solar plexus. The highest center, where one feels the highest *samadhi*, or ecstasy, is in the top of the head. There is a center between the eyebrows. And there is a center in the abdomen, a wonderful center from a physical point of view, because the digestion and assimilation of food is in the center of the

---

1 *The Sufi Message* (1960), vol. 1, pp. 150-52 (abridged).
2 *Sangatha I*, "Tasawwuf/Metaphysics" (privately distributed, abridged).

abdomen, near the navel. The fifth center is in the bottom of man's body. The five centers are called *'arsh, kursi, lauh, kalam,* and *'arsh al-'azam.* The throat center is a semi-center, not a full center; between the shoulder blades there is also a secondary center.[3]

---

3 *Sangatha II,* "Tasawwuf/Metaphysics: The Centers" (privately distributed, abridged).

Five Planes
by Hazrat Inayat Khan

In Sufi terms, there are five stages of consciousness:
Nasut, Malakut, Jabarut, Lahut, Hahut.

1. Nasut. This is the consciousness dependent on our
senses. Whatever we see by means of the eye, or hear by
means of the ear, whatever we smell and taste, all these experiences, which we gain by the help of the material body,
prove to us that this is a particular plane of consciousness,
or a particular kind of experience of consciousness. We call
it Nasut.

2. Malakut. This is a further stage of consciousness,
working through our mental plane. By means of this higher
consciousness we experience thought and imagination,
which are beyond our senses. Very often it happens that a
person does not notice a passerby, so deeply is he thinking
upon some object. You may speak to him, and yet he will
not listen, so deeply is he absorbed in his subject. Though
his ears are open, he cannot hear; though his eyes are open,
he cannot see. What does that mean? It means that at that
moment his consciousness is experiencing life in a different
plane. Though he is sitting before you with open eyes and
ears, his consciousness is on another plane, working through a
different body. This, in Sufi terms, is called Malakut.

124

Spiritual Plane

3. Jabarut. Here the experience is like that of a person in deep, dreamless sleep. He is said to be "sound asleep." The blessing here is greater still. In this higher experience there is God's own Being, by which we experience the life, peace and purity which are within us. Moreover, whilst anyone may experience this blessing during sleep, the person who follows the path of spiritual development will experience it while awake. The Yogis therefore call it *sushupti*, this joy of life and peace and purity, which the mystic experiences with open eyes, while wide awake, though others can only touch it during deep sleep.

The Divine Plane

4. Lahut. This is a still further experience of consciousness. It raises a person from the material plane to the immaterial plane. In this plane the state of being fast asleep is not necessary. There is a greater peace and joy, and nearness to the essence which is called divine. In Christian terms, this stage is called communion. In the Vedantic terms it is called *turiyavastha*. The further step to this is called samadhi, which may, no doubt, be described as merging into God. In other words, in this stage we dive into our deepest self-hood; God is in our deepest self. Here there is the ability to dive so deeply as to touch our deepest being, which is the home of all intelligence, life, peace, and joy; and here worry, fear, disease or death do not enter.

The Transcendent Plane

5. Hahut. This is the experience which is the object of every mystic who follows the inner cult. In Vedantic terms, this stage is called *manan*. The equivalent in Christian terminology is at-one-ment.[1]

---

1 *Supplementary Papers* (privately distributed), "Mysticism II, The Mystery of Sleep II."

The Rhythm of the Heart
by Hazrat Inayat Khan

Whoso believes that the life in the heart means withdrawal from the body does not know the meaning of life. Blood plays a more important part in physical existence than anything else. Thus Sura Ninety-Six begins: "Read in the name of your Lord Who created; He created man from a clot."

Now this has great significance, for it is blood which distinguishes animal from vegetable more than anything else; and in the evolution of higher forms, it is the organization of heart and veins and arteries which becomes most complex. They serve not only the physical body, but make feeling possible. So increase of function in all worlds corresponds to the importance of heart-life in those worlds.

And what is heart? Heart is the seat of life. So Allah has been called the Beneficent and Merciful. The whole life becomes clearer when these processes are understood. It may even be said, there is more of divine energy in those animals where heart is most important; and there is still more divine energy when the consciousness is centered in the heart and bloodstream.

Now peace comes when self is in harmony with the rhythm of the heart. This is accomplished in two ways. In silent meditation all vibrations are stopped, and one enters

126

into the life-stream in the heart; in music, the rhythm and harmony are directed to and through the heart, so that it takes up the proper pulsation.

Everyone knows that all music affects the heart, but such effects may or may not be beneficial. So for many it is not required to exercise this control over the heart, and mastery comes through love and surrender. So if there is any form of concentration to be used in meditation, it consists in first getting into the rhythm of the heart, even though it may be by watching the heartbeats, feeling them and harmonizing with them.

Then one centers all feeling in the physical heart, and out of feeling, selects love; and out of love, divine love. So meditation may be said to begin with a great sweep at the outside of a circle, getting further and further within that circle until one reaches the center of the circle; and at the same time, that very centralizing of attention draws to one all that God has; for to him that gives all to God, Allah bestows whatever is his need.[1]

---

1 *Complete Works of Pir-o-Murshid Hazrat Inayat Khan; 1923 I: January-June* (London and The Hague: East-West Publications and the Nekbakht Foundation, 1989), pp. 307-308: Githa Dhyana Series III, No. 3.

The Twenty Breaths of Purification
by Hazrat Inayat Khan

This exercise must be done without noise or apparent movement in breathing. The finest substance in the air, the essence, ether or *prana*, only is inhaled. The ideal times for this exercise are, from an occult point of view, sunrise and sunset.

During the first three months, the twenty breaths should be felt to reach the solar plexus; during the second three months, they should be felt to reach the navel; during the third three months, the abdominal region; and during the last three months, the base of the spine. The last manner of breathing should be continued during the second year. The rhythm becomes slower and slower every succeeding three months. This exercise should be done standing, preferably outdoors or before an open window.

For nasal catarrh, cleanse with water to which has been added one part soda and two parts salt.

For lung trouble, this exercise should be done in the sunlight, inhaling the rays of the sun.

In this purification practice, there are twenty breaths to be taken in the morning, before food, standing, unless it is prescribed for a person to lie down or sit:

Earth Five breaths in and out through the nostrils.

("Natural breath)

128

Five breaths in through the nostrils and out through the *Wate,*
mouth.

Five breaths in through the mouth and out through the *Fire*
nose.

Five breaths in and out through the mouth. *Air*

Natural breathing is done with the mouth shut; the breaths inhaled and exhaled through the nose are natural breaths. And in this exercise, when the mouth is open, it should be opened only as a little hole, as in whistling.

Special care must be taken not to breathe longer than a normal rhythm. Special attention should be given to stand quite relaxed and in no way force the breath, but to let it find itself its own rhythm.

The exercise is done rhythmically, naturally, without any effort, maintaining the same rhythm throughout (therefore it must not be started too slowly), without movement of the shoulders, and without sound. You are inhaling the subtle thread of air called prana (life, essence of breath; in fact, God Himself) contained in the external air that we feel; and it revivifies, heals, and purifies, nourishing all the invisible centers of the body, those centers through which we experience the spiritual life, and with which we learn to know Spirit. When the technique is mastered, and the breathing done regularly and easily, then practice the exercise faithfully each day, whilst holding the thought and consciousness that you are inhaling the divine essence.

It is not merely a physical exercise (although it helps you to breathe regularly and rhythmically), but it is also for the unfoldment of the soul. It also teaches control and rhythm, and helps you attain a habit of healthy, serene breathing. It is like winding up a clock daily. Begin the day with the exercise, and you will acquire the habit of always breathing rightly. Gradually the idea and consciousness of what you are inhaling with every breath becomes a natural habit, and part of your life. The exercise is the basis of many esoteric exercises and should be mastered before you can understand further mysteries. [1]

---

1 From the papers of the late Halima MacEwan.

Namaz

by Hazrat Inayat Khan

The first step generally taken on this path is namaz, the esoteric prayer, which consists of three objects:

1. Moral Point of View

The building up in one's mind of the God-Ideal, by thought, that the love from the heart may gush forth, making it alive, which ordinarily is as dead. The prayer may be offered by the praise of God's grace and power. The contemplation of divine grace widens the outlook of the devotee and enables him to view, in life, the mercy of God in all aspects; and this produces in him a thankful, contented, resigned, and peaceful nature, which is most essential on this path. The contemplation of divine power discloses before his view the mighty Hand of God working through all things and beings. His justice and rule appear clearly before his eyes, keeping him right and orderly in life.

2. Philosophical Point of View

Prayer in thought only is seldom complete, for a thought in absence of action is considered as no more than an imagination. A thought and action, without speech, are dumb. Therefore, in namaz, while the mind is in contemplation on the thought, the tongue and each organ of the body are busy

131

in prayer at the same time, bowing and prostrating before the grace and power of the Creator. All this, done at one and the same time, keeps man in all planes of existence, engaged in prayer, so that if one plane has escaped it, the other planes drag it back. This makes God see, through the soul of the devotee, the devotion of his heart; and the heart reads the thought of the mind and is moved by it; and the mind listens to the repetitions chanted by the tongue of the devotee; and every atom of the body, conscious of the prayer going through the whole being, realizes itself also, harmoniously joined with the other parts of one's being. The effect is that the whole being of the person becomes exalted by witnessing his absolute being in prayer.

3. Esoteric Point of View

Man exists in two aspects, one real and the other false. The real is the soul, which is the Being of God the Eternal. The other consists of the mind and body, which are composed of borrowed properties of the two planes, the mental and physical, which are bound to be withdrawn in time by the elements to which they belong. And the soul, forgetting this, blinds itself to the false aspect of our being, and loses from sight the thought of the real and everlasting aspect. Therefore, namaz, to the devotee, is a moral culture; to the philosopher, it is a spiritual progress; but to the mystic, it is the first and most essential process to attain to self-realization. [1]

---

1 *Githa I*, "Riyazat, Esotericism, Number 1, Self-Realization" (privately distributed).

Gayatri

by Hazrat Inayat Khan

Every Sufi is free to use the prayer of his own religion, whatever he belongs to, and to observe the form of his own kind of prayer, in private or in public; but if he wishes to use Saum and Salat, prayers which are an answer to the present time, he may use them, with or without movements, once every night before retiring. For some, those of religious attitude, twice a day would be better, but for those who wish for a quicker spiritual evolution, three times would be a good thing.[1]

Saum

Praise be to Thee, Most Supreme God,
Omnipotent, Omnipresent, All-pervading,
the Only Being.
Take us in Thy Parental Arms,
Raise us from the denseness of the earth.
Thy Beauty do we worship,
To Thee do we give willing surrender.
Most Merciful and Compassionate God,
The Idealized Lord of the whole humanity,
Thee only do we worship,
and towards Thee alone we aspire.

---

1 *Sangitha I*, "Namaz" (privately distributed).

Open our hearts towards Thy Beauty,
Illuminate our souls with Divine Light.
O Thou, the Perfection of Love, Harmony and Beauty!
All-powerful Creator, Sustainer, Judge and Forgiver of
our shortcomings,
Lord God of the East and of the West,
of the worlds above and below,
And of the seen and unseen beings.
Pour upon us Thy Love and Thy Light,
Give sustenance to our bodies, hearts and souls,
Use us for the purpose that Thy Wisdom chooseth,
And guide us on the path of Thine Own Goodness.
Draw us closer to Thee every moment of our life,
Until in us be reflected Thy Grace,
Thy Glory, Thy Wisdom, Thy Joy and Thy Peace.
Amen.

Salat

Most gracious Lord,
Master, Messiah, and Savior of humanity,
We greet Thee with all humility.
Thou art the First Cause and the Last Effect,
the Divine Light and the Spirit of Guidance,
Alpha and Omega.
Thy Light is in all forms,
Thy Love in all beings:
in a loving mother, in a kind father, in an innocent child,
in a helpful friend, in an inspiring teacher.
Allow us to recognize Thee in all
Thy holy names and forms:
as Rama, as Krishna, as Shiva, as Buddha.
Let us know Thee as Abraham, as Solomon, as
Zarathushtra, as Moses, as Jesus, as Mohammed,
and in many other names and forms, known and
unknown to the world.
We adore Thy past,

134

Thy presence deeply enlighteneth our being,
and we look for Thy blessing in the future.
Messenger, Christ, Nabi, the Rasul of God!
Thou Whose heart constantly reacheth upward,
Thou comest on earth with a Message,
as a dove from above when Dharma decayeth,
and speakest the Word that is put into Thy mouth,
as the light filleth the crescent moon.
Let the star of the Divine Light shining in Thy heart
be reflected in the hearts of Thy devotees.
May the Message of God reach far and wide,
illuminating and making the whole humanity
as one single Brotherhood in the Fatherhood of God.
Amen.[2]

Khatum

Thou, Who art the Perfection of Love, Harmony, and Beauty,
The Lord of heaven and earth,
open our hearts, that we may hear Thy Voice,
which constantly cometh from within.
Disclose to us Thy Divine Light,
which is hidden in our souls,
that we may know and understand life better.
Most Merciful and Compassionate God,
give us Thy great Goodness,
Teach us Thy loving Forgiveness,
Raise us above the distinctions and differences
which divide men,[3]
Send us the Peace of Thy Divine Spirit,
And unite us all in Thy Perfect Being.
Amen.

---

2 In practice, the Sufi Order International and Sufi Ruhaniat International substitute the more inclusive phrase, "one single Family in the Parenthood of God," for, "one single Brotherhood in the Fatherhood of God." Both Orders also have additional prayers in which female exemplars are named.
3 The S.O.I. replaces "men" with "us"; the S.R.I. omits it.

Pir

Inspirer of my mind, consoler of my heart,
healer of my spirit,
Thy presence lifteth me from earth to heaven,
Thy words flow as the sacred river,
Thy thought riseth as a divine spring,
Thy tender feelings waken sympathy in my heart.
Beloved Teacher, Thy very being is forgiveness.
The clouds of doubt and fear are scattered
by Thy piercing glance.
All ignorance vanishes in Thy illuminating presence.
A new hope is born in my heart by breathing
Thy peaceful atmosphere.
O inspiring Guide through life's puzzling ways,
In Thee I feel abundance of blessing.
Amen.

Nabi

A torch in the darkness, a staff during my weakness,
A rock in the weariness of life,
Thou, my Master, makest earth a paradise.
Thy thought giveth me unearthly joy,
Thy light illuminateth my life's path,
Thy words inspire me with divine wisdom,
I follow in thy footsteps,
which lead me to the eternal goal.
Comforter of the broken-hearted,
Support of those in need,
Friend of the lovers of truth,
Blessed Master, thou art the Prophet of God.
Amen.

Rasul

Warner of coming dangers,
Wakener of the world from sleep,
Deliverer of the Message of God,
Thou art our Savior.
The sun at the dawn of Creation,
The light of the whole universe,
The fulfillment of God's purpose,
Thou, the life eternal, we seek refuge
in Thy loving enfoldment.
Spirit of Guidance,
Source of all beauty, and Creator of harmony,
Love, Lover, and Beloved Lord.
Thou art our divine ideal.
Amen.

Prayer of the Universel

O Thou, who art the Maker, Molder
and Builder of the universe,
build with Thine own hands
the Universel,
our temple for Thy divine Message
of Love, Harmony and Beauty.
Amen.

Nayaz

Beloved Lord, Almighty God!
Through the rays of the sun,
Through the waves of the air,
Through the All-pervading Life in space,
Purify and revivify me, and I pray,
Heal my body, heart, and soul.
Amen.

Nazar

O Thou, the Sustainer of our bodies, hearts, and souls,
Bless all that we receive in thankfulness.
Amen.

The Rules
by Hazrat Inayat Khan

Iron Rules

My conscientious self:

Make no false claims.

Speak not against others in their absence.

Do not take advantage of a person's ignorance.

Do not boast of your good deeds.

Do not claim that which belongs to another.

Do not reproach others, making them firm in their faults.

Do not spare yourself in the work which you must
accomplish.

Render your services faithfully to all who require them.

Seek not profit by putting someone in straits.

Harm no one for your own benefit.

Copper Rules

My conscientious self:

Consider your responsibility sacred.

Be polite to all.

Do nothing which will make your conscience feel guilty.

Extend your help willingly to those in need.

Do not look down upon the one who looks up to you.

Judge not another by your own law.

Bear no malice against your worst enemy.

Influence no one to do wrong.

Be prejudiced against no one.

Prove trustworthy in all your dealings.

Silver Rules

My conscientious self:

Consider duty as sacred as religion.

Use tact on all occasions.

Place people rightly in your estimation.

Be no more to anyone than you are expected to be.

Have regard for the feelings of every soul.

Do not challenge anyone who is not your equal.

Do not make a show of your generosity.

Do not ask a favor of those who will not grant it you.

Meet your shortcomings with a sword of self-respect.

Let not your spirit be humbled in adversity.

Golden Rules

My conscientious self:

Keep to your principles in prosperity as well as in adversity.

Be firm in faith through life's tests and trials.

Guard the secrets of friends as your most sacred trust.

Observe constancy in love.

Break not your word of honor whatever may befall.

Meet the world with smiles in all conditions of life.

When you possess something, think of the one who does not possess it.

Uphold your honor at any cost.

Hold your ideal high in all circumstances.

Do not neglect those who depend upon you.

WORDS AND MELODIES

Sayings
by Hazrat Inayat Khan

Make God a reality, and God will make you the truth.

O peace-maker, before trying to make peace throughout the world, first make peace within thyself!

A pure conscience gives one the strength of lions, and by a guilty conscience even lions are turned into rabbits.

The closer one approaches reality, the nearer one comes to unity.

Do not weep with the sad, but console them; if not, by your tears you will but water the plant of their sorrow.

Pleasure blocks, but pain clears the way of inspiration.

The fountain stream of love rises in the love for an individual, but spreads and falls in universal love.

A tender-hearted sinner is better than a saint hardened by piety.

The secret of all success is strength of conviction.

A worldly loss often turns into spiritual gain.

Optimism is the result of love.

The truly great souls become streams of love.

When the soul is attuned to God every action becomes music.

The key to all happiness is the love of God.

Be sparing of your words if you wish them to be powerful.

Divinity is human perfection and humanity is divine limitation.

Behind us is one spirit and one life; how then can we be happy if our neighbor is sad?

Life itself becomes a scripture to the kindled soul.

Every moment of your life is more valuable than anything else.

A pure life and a clean conscience are as bread and wine for the soul.

Overlook the greatest fault in another, but do not partake of it to the smallest degree.

The pain of life is the price paid for the quickening of the heart.

Spirituality is the tuning of the heart; one can obtain it neither by study, nor by piety.

Right and wrong depend upon attitude and situation, not upon the action.

Failure in life does not matter; the greatest misfortune is standing still.

There is nothing we take in this bazaar of life that we shall not sooner or later have to pay for.

The service of God means that we each work for all.

Every virtue is but an expression of beauty.

The water that washes the heart is the continual running of the love-stream.

Life is what it is; you cannot change it, but you can change yourself.

Speech is the sign of the living; but silence is life itself.

All that is from God is for all souls.

The Sufi's tendency is to look at everything from two points of view: from his own and that of another.

Natural religion is the religion of beauty.

The same light which is fire on earth and the sun in the sky, is God in heaven.

All surrender to beauty willingly and to power unwillingly.

The hidden desire of the Creator is the secret of the whole Creation.

The true ego is born of the ashes of the false.

Sympathy breaks the congestion of the heart.

To repress desire is to suppress a divine impulse.

With trust in God, with goodwill, self-confidence, and a
hopeful attitude towards life, man will always win his
battle, however difficult.

If anyone strikes my heart, it does not break, but it bursts;
and the flame coming out of it becomes a torch on my
path.

Let me grow quietly in Thy garden as a speechless plant,
that some day my flowers and fruits may sing the legend of
my silent past.

Spiritual attainment is attuning oneself to a higher pitch.

The path of freedom leads to the goal of captivity; it is the
path of discipline which leads to the goal of liberty.

To an angelic soul, love means glorification; to a jinn soul,
love means admiration; to a human soul, love means
affection; to an animal soul, love means passion.

Love that ends is the shadow of love; true love is without
beginning or end.

It is death which dies, not life.

A virtue carried too far may become a sin.

Souls unite at the meeting of a glance.

Shatter your ideals upon the rock of truth.

If you will not rise above the things of this world, they will
rise above you.

What limits God? His name.

Prayer is a deep-felt need of the soul.

In the union of two loving hearts is the Unity of God.

Nothing that your mind can conceive, does not exist.

The best way to love is to serve.

If belief is a thing, faith is a living being.

Do I pass through life? No, it is life that passes by me.

The day you feel you do not know, you will begin to know.

There is nothing more subtle or simpler than truth.

Food is the nourishment of the body; thought is a refreshment to the mind; love is the subsistence for the heart; truth is the sustenance of the soul.

In the drop, the sea is as small as the drop; in the sea, a drop is as large as the sea.

Perfection is attained by five achievements: life, light, power, happiness, and peace.

Peace will not come to a lover's heart so long as he will not become love itself.

The Message is a call to those whose hour has come to awake, and it is a lullaby to those who are still meant to sleep.

The essence of today's Message is balance.

To discover the heart is the greatest initiation.

Divinity is the exaltation of the human soul.

The one who seeks the spiritual path is sought after by the spirit.

The more you depend upon God, the more God becomes dependable.

Love's reward is love itself.[1]

---

1 Selected from *The Sufi Message of Hazrat Inayat Khan: Gayan, Vadan, Nirtan* (London: Barrie and Rockliff, 1960).

Ragas and Gamakas
by Hazrat Inayat Khan

Beloved, Thou makest me fuller every day.
Thou diggest into my heart deeper than the depths of the earth.
Thou raisest my soul higher than the highest heaven,
making me more empty every day and yet fuller.
Thou makest me wider than the ends of the world;
Thou stretchest my two arms across the land and the sea,
giving into my enfoldment the East and the West.
Thou changest my flesh into fertile soil;
Thou turnest my blood into streams of water;
Thou kneadest my clay, I know, to make a new universe.

Let Thy wish become my desire,
Let Thy will become my deed,
Let Thy word become my speech, Beloved,
And Thy love become my creed.

Let my plant bring forth Thy flowers,
Let my fruits produce Thy seed,
Let my heart become Thy lute, Beloved,
And my body Thy flute of reed.

Why have I two eyes if not to behold Thy glorious vision?
Why have I two ears if not to hear Thy gentle whisper?
Why have I the sense of smell if not to breathe the essence
of Thy spirit?
Why have I two lips, Beloved, if not to kiss Thy beautiful
countenance?
Why have I two hands if not to work in Thy divine cause?
Why have I two legs if not to walk in Thy spiritual path?
Why have I a voice if not to sing Thy celestial song?
Why have I a heart, Beloved, if not to make it Thy sacred
dwelling?

Every step in Thy path draws me nearer to Thee,
Every breath in Thy thought exhilarates my spirit,
Every glimpse of Thy smile is inspiring to my soul,
Every tear in Thy love, Beloved, exalts my being.

Why, O my feeling heart
Do you live and die?
What makes my feeling heart
To laugh and to cry?
Death is my life indeed;
I live when I die.
Pain is my pleasure; when
I laugh, then I cry.

⌁

Before you judge my actions,
Lord, I pray, you will forgive.
Before my heart has broken,
Will you help my soul to live?
Before my eyes are covered,
Will you let me see your face?
Before my feet are tired,
May I reach your dwelling place?
Before I wake from slumber,
You will watch me, Lord, I hold.
Before I throw my mantle,
Will you take me in your fold?
Before my work is over,
You, my Lord, will right the wrong.
Before you play your music,
Will you let me sing my song?[1]

---

1 Selected from *The Sufi Message of Hazrat Inayat Khan: Gayan, Vadan, Nirtan* (London: Barrie and Rockliff, 1960).

Sufi Songs

Sung Zikr

Hazrat Inayat Khan

la e la ha el al la__ hu la e la ha el al la__ hu

la e la ha el al la__ hu la e la ha el al la__ hu

el al la____ hu el al la__ hu

al la____ hu al la____ hu

hu hu

Original version of 1921

la e la ha el al la__ hu la e la ha el al la__ hu

la e la ha el al la__ hu la e la ha el al la__ hu

154

Thy Wish

Hazrat Inayat Khan (words from the Vadan)

Maheboob Khan

Song to the Madzub (op. 40)

Pirzadi Noor-un-Nisa Inayat Khan

4

Prayer of Invocation

as sung by Inayat Khan

Prayer of Invocation

Praise to Thee, Who art hidden & yet manifest.
Praise to Thy Glory, Might, Power & Dominion,
To Whom belong all Majesty & Greatness,
Who art the source of all things.
Praise to Thee, King of Kings,
Ruler of all Creation,
Who controlleth all things and hast
power over all things.
Thou who wast from the beginning,
and art without end, for ever and for ever,
Who art eternal, above all, beyond all.
O God, Lord and Ruler over angels
and mankind.

ACTIVITIES AND INITIATIVES

Brotherhood[1]

The work of this activity is to throw the inner light upon different aspects of life, such as art, music, poetry, drama, education, history, social reform, and comparative religion; that thereby, through whatever walk of life, we may make our way to life's destination, creating that sympathetic attitude towards one another, which may result in mutual harmony, culminating in a world peace.[2]

Behind all this world of various names and forms there is one life, there is one spirit. This spirit, which is the soul of all beings, is attracted towards unity; and it is the absence of this spirit which keeps the world unhappy. To a person who has just had some unpleasantness with his brother or sister, his food is tasteless, the night without sleep, the heart restless, the soul under a cloud. This shows that we do not necessarily live on food; our soul lives on love, the love that we receive and the love that we give. The absence of this love is our unhappiness, and the presence of it is all we need. Nothing in the

---

1 Brotherhood is now called Brotherhood-Sisterhood in the International Sufi Movement, and Kinship in the Sufi Order International.
2 *The Sufi Movement* (Southampton, England: The Sufi Movement, n.d.), p. 5.

world is a greater healing power, a greater remedy, a greater happiness, than to be conscious of brotherhood.

Brotherhood is not something which is learned or taught. Brotherhood is a tendency, a tendency which arises from a heart that is tuned to a proper pitch. And it is in this natural tendency that the real happiness lies, from which rises harmony, and which culminates in peace. The Message of brotherhood is a message of sympathy, a message of harmony.

We do not wish all the people in the world to be of the same religion or the same education, or to have the same customs and manners; nor do we think that all classes must become one class, which is impossible anyhow. We wish that all classes may blend with each other, and yet every individual may have his own individual expression in life; that all nations may have their peculiarity, their individuality, but at the same time express goodwill and friendly feeling towards one another; that different races may have their own manners and their own ideas, but at the same time understand one another; that the followers of different religions may continue to belong to their own religions, but at the same time become tolerant towards each other.

It is not at all the mission of the Sufi Movement to try and make the whole of humanity followers of one special movement, but to give to humanity what God has given us, so that we may serve in His cause.[3]

---

3 *The Sufi Message* (1964), vol. 10, pp. 265-270 (abridged).

Universal Worship

The devotional activity of the Sufi Movement is to recognize the divine wisdom in all its forms of diversity of faiths and beliefs; and to respect the illuminated souls who have drawn their inspiration from one and the same source, the divine Spirit of Guidance, in order to help humanity, at different periods, in various lands, in their time of need.

Not only do we acknowledge this ideal by the feeling of worship when entering any of the many mansions of the Lord, by looking with veneration on the inspired teachers of the world, and by studying different scriptures in reverence; but we also acknowledge this idea by placing on God's altar the scriptures of all accepted religions, and lighting candles in the name of all the illuminated souls, known and unknown to the world, thus making our service a Universal Worship.

There is also a formless service of the Universal Worship, which is free of any kind of ceremonial, so that these two ways of worship may meet the need of those who like ritual and those who prefer a service without it.

The devotional side of the Movement is not for any particular sect or religion; it is a Church of All, as it includes all churches, and in order to follow it, no one need give up his own way of worship.[1]

---

1 *The Sufi Movement* (n.d.), pp. 6-7.

Basic beliefs of Universal Worship

1. The existence of One God, the God of all.

2. All teachers of humanity who have guided humanity towards the ideal have been an embodiment of the divine Spirit of Guidance.

3. Humanity needs to be brought to that consciousness of unity which is the central theme of all religions.

Basic principles of Universal Worship

1. To have regard for all teachers of humanity.
2. To feel respect for all the religious scriptures.
3. To give an earnest response to the Sufi Message.
4. To grant full allegiance to the Seraj-un-Munir.
5. Not to criticize any existing religion.
6. Not to antagonize those holding an opposite opinion.
7. Not to influence others to leave any faith or belief for Universal Worship.

The Sunday Service

There is a flame burning above the altar, before the doors of the church are opened. Incense is burning on the altar, which is adorned with flowers. Six candles stand on the altar in the form of a crescent, each representing one of the great world religions.

Between the third and fourth candles, but just a little more in front and beneath the light which represents God (i.e. the flame burning above the altar), stands a candle, representing the Spirit of Guidance. In front of this taller candle the incense is burning, and before this lies the *Gayan, Vadan,* or *Nirtan.* The scriptures belonging to the six world religions lie at the foot of the six different candles, in the following order from right to left (the right being the right of the altar).

1. Hindu religion.
2. Buddhist religion.
3. Zoroastrian religion.
4. Hebrew religion.
5. Christian religion
6. Religion of Islam.

When the Cherags enter, all present rise and stand until the Cherags have taken their seats. The Cherag giving the sermon goes to the chair at the left of the altar, the two other Cherags sit opposite him on the right.

The Cherag who lights the candles rises, lights the taper from the burning flame and, standing at the right side of the altar, says, lifting the taper with both hands and facing the burning light:

"Toward the One, the Perfection of Love, Harmony and Beauty, the Only Being, united with all the Illuminated Souls, who form the Embodiment of the Master, the Spirit of Guidance."

He then kindles the first, the second and the third candles; and then goes to the other side of the altar and kindles from that side the fourth, fifth, and sixth candles, each time saying:

"To the glory of the Omnipresent God we kindle the light symbolically representing . . . . (1. the Hindu religion; 2. the Buddhist religion; 3. the Zoroastrian religion; 4. the Hebrew religion; 5. the Christian religion; 6. The religion of Islam)."

When the Cherag says: "We kindle the light," he actually lights the candle, and does not proceed till after the candle has been kindled.

After this the Cherag lights the candle representing the Spirit of Guidance, standing at the left corner of the altar and saying, "To the glory of the Omnipresent God we kindle the light symbolically representing all those who, whether known or unknown to the world, have held aloft the Light of Truth through the darkness of human ignorance."

Extinguishing the taper, he hands it over to the Cherag sitting in that corner, who lays it down. He then turns to the congregation saying, "Let us pray"; and turning his face to the burning light hanging above the altar, and still standing at the left corner of the altar, says Saum, while all stand.

The Cherag then resumes his seat and all sit down. Then the Cherag reading the scriptures rises, and standing at the right corner of the altar says to the congregation: "We will read from the world scriptures."

He then proceeds in the same way as the Cherag who lighted the candles, reading the six scriptures one after the other. Taking the first book, he opens it, facing the congregation, and says: "We read in the Hindu scriptures."

Having read this book he shuts it and, after turning to the burning light, he raises the book with both hands, saying:

"We offer to the Omniscient God, our reverence, our homage and our gratitude, for the Light of the Divine Wisdom."

In the same way he proceeds with the two other scriptures, saying then: "For the Light of the Divine *Compassion*. . . . of the Divine *Purity*."

He then walks to the other side of the altar and takes the books of the Hebrew religion, Christian religion and Islam from that corner, ending: "For the Light of the Divine *Law* . . . . Divine Self-sacrifice . . . . Divine *Unity*."

After the reading of the scriptures the Cherag says: "We will now have a few minutes silence."

After the silence (about three minutes), the Cherag rises, and standing at the right corner of the altar, says: "Let us pray." All present rise. After the Cherag has said Salat, the two other Cherags and the congregation sit down, but he goes to the altar, takes the *Gayan*, *Vadan* or *Nirtan*, and standing at the right corner of the altar, opens it and reads. After the reading he shuts it and proceeds as in the case of the other scriptures, saying: "We offer . . . . for the Light of the Divine *Truth*."

He then takes his seat, and the Cherag who gives the sermon (which may be a *Gatheka*) rises. After the sermon he says the Khatum, facing the burning light from the left corner of the altar.

After this he turns to the middle of the altar, and facing the congregation, he gives the blessing. Raising his arms in benediction he says:

"May the blessing of God rest upon you; may His peace abide with you; and may His presence illuminate your heart, now and for evermore. Amen."[2]

The Cherags leave the church in the same way in which they entered it.

Music may be included in the service at the discretion of the Seraj.

Collections may be taken at the door as the congregation leaves the church.[3]

An Account of the First Universal Worship Service
By Shabaz Mitchell

It is not easy to write one's impressions of the ceremony which took place at No. 35 Tregunter Road, London, on the evening of Saturday, May 7th, 1921.

From the world of hurrying crowds, motor buses and taxi cabs, of violent activity, noise and confusion, one passes into a tall Georgian house. Here, by comparison, the atmosphere seems at first to be one of profound peace; people move about quietly and speak in subdued tones; but it is a peace full of expectancy, for an event is awaited.

One is invited upstairs into a room on the first floor. As the door is opened, one's eyes first catch a glimpse of a lighted

2 In the Sufi Order International the following form is used: "May the blessing of God rest upon you; may God's peace abide with you; and may God's presence illuminate your heart, now and for everymore. Amen."

3 *Universal Worship* (Geneva: International Headquarters of the Sufi Movement, 1936), pp. 3-12 (abridged).

candle and the smoke of burning incense upon an improvised altar. On both sides of the room, facing one another, are to be seen double rows of chairs occupied by one's fellow mureeds, some of them well-known friends, others strangers. Music is being played on an American organ; the scene resembles that of a chancel in a private chapel.

During a wait of half an hour one notices many small things; the contagion of the crowds, the effect of hurry, the impression of the score of small irritating incidents cling about one. One also becomes aware that others too, have their disturbing thoughts and emotions; for although there is little sound in this room, the atmosphere is as an unquiet sea.

It seems that we have waited a long time when the music ceases, the door opens and Murshid enters. His presence alters everything; all rise as he comes in, and he passes between the double rows of standing mureeds to a seat near the altar; then we sit down once more.

Presently, Murshid, who is wearing his black robe, rises and begins to speak. He explains the value of devotion; the importance of prayer; how none, even the most intellectual, can afford to dispense with their aid; how ritual, though not a necessity to spiritual progress, may yet be a help. The hour, he says, has come when it is desirable that a firmer prayer shall be used in connection with the Sufi Order.

By now beautiful influences have filled the little room, and the sea of thoughts and feelings is, at last, so it seems, at peace. Then for the first time the mureeds hear the form of prayer, which in future is to be used at such Sufi services, the form in which essential ideas behind the Sufi teaching are embodied.

Murshid stands facing his mureeds, and Miss Dowland, the National Representative, on his left hand, begins to read the prayers in a calm, strong voice. As she reads, Murshid, with closed eyes, makes gently and with deliberation, the appropriate gestures, his movements being watched by all with indescribable emotion. The prayers themselves are the most comprehensive we have ever listened to; they lift the thoughts to things above and turn them on things beneath. They speak of the greatness, the power, the beauty, the all-pervadingness of God, also of His messengers, Rama, Krishna, Buddha, Abraham, Zoroaster, Moses, Jesus, Muhammad and "those whose names are unknown."

In the accompanying gestures are represented signs, which have come down through the ages and are especially associated with each of the great world religions: the upraised palms characteristic of Islam, the downward sweeping gesture of Hinduism, the sign of the cross of Christianity, and many others.

As one looks, one's heart melts with desire to experience some reflection of that realization which lends such meaning to the deep inclination before the vision of irresistible beauty, the face covered by the hands at the thought of peace.

The prayers finished, Murshid leaves us. He is gone what seems to be a very long time. When he returns, he is preceded by Miss Sophia E.M. Green, who carries in her hand an unlighted candle; she walks with concentrated thoughts, towards the altar, and kneels on a cushion at Murshid's feet. Bending towards her, Murshid with his finger inscribes invisible characters upon her forehead, then sets a seal upon her forehead with the palm of his hand, lays his hands on the crown of her head, declaring her to be ordained in the Church of All, with power to illuminate herself and others. We hold our breath, realizing it is a moment of profound significance. He next lights a taper at the tall candle burning on the altar, and with this sets light to the candle which Miss Green is holding; then he helps her to rise and invests her with the black silk robe of her office. Thus is the first cheraga ordained in the Church of All.

During this part of the ceremonial, feelings of love and sympathy flow out from many of the mureeds towards Miss

Green, whose great honor and great responsibility they appreciate.

Then comes the reception into the Church of All of six of the mureeds present. They file out of the room, returning each holding an unlit candle; they in turn kneel before the newly ordained cheraga who, by writing upon their foreheads, by laying her hand upon the crown of their head, by repeating the sentences previously spoken by Murshid, and by lighting each candle from her candle, receives each in turn.

In this ritual, to the onlooker, there is something profoundly touching, for are not these the first seven? They file up to Murshid, receive his blessing with bowed heads, and place their candles upon the altar, so that now the number of lighted candles, including the tallest of which Murshid has made use, is eight.

The other mureeds, who up to the present have been merely spectators, now fall in behind their received brethren and each in turn receives the blessing of Murshid.

The final scene consists of a recital by the cheraga, in Murshid's absence, of the prayers with the accompanying gestures. She faces the altar for the purpose, and the whole company also face the altar, the mureeds repeating the gestures in silence.

And when the little company disperses to pass into the London night, the thought in one's mind is that there has just been planted a tiny seed, which shall one day spring up into a great tree whose leaves shall be for the healing of the nation.[4]

---

4 From a paper in the Nekbakht Foundation Archive.

Spiritual Healing

Its purpose: to awaken humanity to a greater realization of the power of the divine spirit to heal, thus to bring about a better state of physical, mental and spiritual health, and so to fulfill the law of God.[1]

Spiritual healing can be performed by a single being, as well as by a group of people. In this case, the heart of the healer can send forth its feelings and vibrations, and, in accordance with their intensity, the subject is healed. In absent spiritual healing, the desire spreads forth its rays and reaches the patient wherever he may be, curing him without the presence of the healer. The concentration of several people united together works still more wonderfully.[2]

The Healing Service

Preparation for the Service

The leader sits at a little table covered with a yellow cloth, which is embroidered with the Sufi emblem, the winged heart with crescent and star; the symbolism of the emblem being:

---

1 Hazrat Inayat Khan, from a paper in the Archive of the Nekbakht Foundation.
2 Hazrat Inayat Khan, *The Sufi Message* (1961), vol. 4, p. 93.

"Verily, the heart responsive to the light of God is liberated." There should also be on the table a bowl of flowers, symbol of life; a piece of amber, symbol of magnetism; and a glass of water, symbol of purity; also, burning incense, symbol of prayer rising to God.

The other members of the group sit with the leader in a circle. It is to be recommended, at the beginning of the meeting, to read from the book *Health*.

Before the service starts, the leader will do well to read the names of the patients and ask if anyone present has got some information of them, and also if someone proposes a new patient to be taken up. It is recommended that, when known, the maiden name of the patient is mentioned with the surname. It is suggested that the patients should be asked whether they wish to be placed on the list. A person who is seriously ill is advised to refrain from participating. Should it be the intention of someone to attend the ceremony in order to be healed himself, he is also requested to refrain from participating, and to give his name as a patient on the list.

A leader should, as a rule, start with three or five members of the group (the leader included), which number can increase later. The leader of the group should be a mureed; among the members non-mureeds may be taken up. As a rule, the number of patients should be limited to ten.

The service consists of three sections, all three consisting of: "invocation—silence—prayer—pause." After the third section the actual healing takes place. While concentrating on the patient, one should see him in perfect health before one. If the patient is not known, one should keep the sound of his name in one's ears. Throughout this last part of the ceremony, the leader of the group concentrates on the healing power of God. The members of the group keep in mind that they do not heal the patient themselves, but that God does this through them.

Healing Service

Invocation (by the leader):
Toward the One, the Perfection of Love, Harmony, and Beauty, the Only Being, united with all the Illuminated souls, who form the Embodiment of the Master, the Spirit of Guidance.

Silence (a few minutes):
During this silence one may concentrate on the peace and unity of the whole creation.

Prayer (by the leader):
O Thou, Whose nature is mercy and compassion, and Whose being is all-peace, Father, Creator, and Sustainer of our lives, send on the whole humanity Thy peace, and unite us all in Thy divine harmony. Amen.

Pause.

Invocation (by the leader):
Toward the One... (During this second invocation all are standing, forming a closed chain by joining hands, each holding his right hand on the top of the left of his neighbor. After the invocation all sit down again.)

Silence (a few minutes):
During this silence one may concentrate on being used as a channel.

Prayer (by the leader):
O Thou, who art the Spirit of our souls, the Master of our minds and the Controller of our bodies, we most humbly offer Thee ourselves to be used as channels of Thy love, light and life, that we may be more able to serve Thee and humanity. Amen.

Pause.

Invocation (by the leader):
Toward the One...

Silence (a few minutes):
During this silence one may concentrate on the stream of the divine healing power, flowing through us.

Prayer (by the leader):
O Thou, the Light of all souls, the Life of all beings, the Healer of our hearts, All-sufficient and All-powerful God, the Forgiver of our shortcomings, free us from all pain and suffering, and make us Thine instruments, that we may in turn free others from pain and suffering, and we may impart to them Thy light, Thy life, Thy joy and Thy peace. Amen.

Pause.

The names of the patients are read by the leader or by someone appointed by him. After each name is mentioned the leader should breathe five times: inhaling *Shafi* (the healing power of God), exhaling *Kafi* (the all-pervading life of God). After that the leader says the Healing Prayer.

Healing Prayer:
O Thou, the Healer of our bodies, hearts, and souls, by Thy mercy may he/she be healed, by Thy all-sufficient power of healing. Amen.

After the ten names have been called the leader says: "We shall hold a silence for all those, whose names have not been mentioned, but also need healing." Then the leader should breathe again, five times, Shafi-Kafi, after which he says the second Healing Prayer.

Second Healing Prayer:
O Thou, the Healer of our bodies, hearts, and souls, may by Thy mercy and by Thy all-sufficient power of healing all others, known to us, whose names and needs Thou knowest, be healed. Amen.

Silence, after which all rise. The prayer Khatum may follow here (according to the discretion of the healing leader). When the leader says, "Amen," all draw their hands over their face downwards. In case Khatum is not said, after the silence all rise and also draw their hands over their face downwards.[3]

Service for the Upliftment of the Sick

Arrange eight candles as in the Church of All. Have flowers, water, incense burning, sandalwood, amber, and symbol.

Let patient sit, or lie on bed or couch.

The officiant shall first light the six candles representing the great masters who have brought the Message of God at different periods in the history of the world. As each candle is lit, he shall invoke the aid of the master who is represented by that candle: Rama, Buddha, Zoroaster, Moses, Jesus, Muhammad. Then he shall light the candle representing the Spirit of Guidance.

Silence.

The officiant shall stand and repeat Saum.

Silence.

The officiant shall stand and repeat the following prayer: O Thou, the Almighty Sun Whose Light cleareth away all clouds, we pray Thee disperse the mists of illusion and ease the life of Thy worshippers by Thy all-sufficient healing power, and by the Grace of the Illuminated Souls who form the embodiment of the Master, the Spirit of Guidance. Pour on us Thy limitless Love, Thy shining Light, Thy everlasting Life, Thy heavenly Joy and Thy Perfect Peace. Amen.[4]

---

3 Authorized version dated May 22, 1963, in the Archive of the Nekbakht Foundation. Other versions of the service existed in Murshid's time, and additional variations have since been introduced.
4 From a paper in the Archive of the Nekbakht Foundation.

Ziraat

Ziraat is a continuation of the ancient mysteries. The ceremonies and teachings of Ziraat are based upon the law of harmony underlying all the workings of nature as applied to agriculture. Initiates of Ziraat are the workers whose duty it is to be the custodians guarding the sanctity of the Earth.[1]

The spiritual life is given in Ziraat as a seed. In Ziraat the person digs in the ground and cultivates the heart to find out its real essence, its inspiration, and its life. He cultivates the power to make spiritual life out of everyday life. The whole secret of Ziraat is in this: "What is the seed?" The seed is spiritual life itself. The seed is the life of the Messenger. As a seed, it grows in your heart and, from there, it changes humanity and society, and makes all things new; it grows out in a new, a reborn man, who is to live forever.

The first work of the ploughman is self-analysis. Once self-analysis is made, he has brought from the soil of his mind to the surface all that was there, that nothing good or bad remains buried there. By cultivation of mind, when all the foreign element is rooted out, the mind becomes pure, and man becomes his own self.

1 *The Sufi Order* (New Lebanon, New York: Sufi Order Publications, 1979), p. 15 (abridged).

To renew the mind and, at the same time, to renew life as its result, is the goal of toiling on the farm. The symbol of this toiling is the plough, with which the laborer works the soil of his mind, thus making the ground free from every kind of root and stone, making it softer and smoother, almost ready to sow the seed.

Ploughing is done in the first degree. In further degrees, one sows and one reaps. As the ritual says: farming consists mainly of three kinds of work: ploughing, sowing, reaping. "We plough with toil, we sow with hope, and we reap with joy."

Greeting the elements is done, because all that has become manifested is the result of the elements, and such is the mind. The elements are the primitive manifestations, in other words, an immediate expression of God. And so is the pure mind an immediate expression of God. The elements are the living entities which make our mind. If we make them pure, the mind becomes a pure reflection and an immediate expression of God.

The central point to be considered in Ziraat is the profiting from this life, which is a farm of God, by exploring it, cultivating it, and making it fertile, in which is accomplished the purpose of the manifestation.[2]

---

2 From the paper "Additional Pages to Ziraat: Heard from Murshid by Sirdar" in the Nekbakht Archive.

The Universel

Hazrat Inayat Khan laid the foundation stone for the Universel on September 13, 1926, the last day he was amongst his disciples in the West. He chose a site on a field in Suresnes, France, on the slopes of Mt. Valerien, originally the Mount of Hermits, overlooking Paris. It had been the seat of a Druid temple and was a place of pilgrimage, as well as a healing center where Sainte Geneviève, the patron saint of Paris, discovered a source of water.[1]

In 1969, the Sufi Movement erected a Universel temple in Katwijk, Holland, beside the dune Murshid named Murad Hasil, "the place of wish fulfillment." Two decades later Pir Vilayat established a Universel chapel in the garden of Fazal Manzil in Suresnes. Universel temples have also sprung up in Cape Town, South Africa, and Bothell, Washington (U.S.A.).

The Universel is not only a physical house of worship; it is also an inner akasha. Murshid explained:

"This is where God's Message will be treasured, a temple in which the future generations will find what they seek. And how is it designed, and how is it to be constructed? It is designed by the hand of God, and it is to be constructed by

1 *The Sufi Order* (1979), p. 10.

our thoughts of harmony, of love, of beauty. It is our thoughts and our feelings which will serve in this temple as stones and bricks and tiles, and it is our feelings which will hold this temple for centuries to come."[2]

---

2 *The Message Papers* (privately distributed), p. 24 (July 21, 1925).

The Confraternity

On the occasion of the laying of the foundation stone of the Universel, Hazrat Inayat Khan founded the Confraternity of the Message, an order within the Universal Worship, whose members pledge themselves to build, with their prayers, the inner Universel in the higher spheres, in anticipation of its materialization on the physical plane.[1]

The Confraternity was formed by Hazrat Inayat Khan, the first seraj-un-munir, to provide a method by which sincere and devoted members of the Universal Worship may unite in a daily form of prayer for spreading the Message.

It is divided into two parts called:

1. The Duty
2. The Task

The first is obligatory upon all who join; the second is voluntary. The form of both is given below.

The Duty

To repeat at sunrise, or upon waking, the prayer Saum; "May the Message of God spread far and wide" (101 times); and the prayer Pir.

---

1 The Sufi Order (1979), p. 10.

To repeat at noon the prayer Salat; "Pour on us Thy love and Thy light" (101 times); and the prayer Nabi.

To repeat at sunset the prayer Khatum; "Disclose to us Thy divine light" (101 times); and the prayer Rasul.

A sacred vow to fulfill these devotions will be taken with the seraj-un-munir, or the seraj of the country, by the candidate for membership in the confraternity of the Message.

Note. When there is a church or chapel of the Universal Worship, these devotions may all be done at one hour as a form of collective worship; in this case the candle of the Message should be kindled from the center light, and the words repeated aloud by each person at the same time. The ribbon and medal of the Confraternity should be worn at a collective devotion, and also for the hours.

The Task

The Task, which may be undertaken voluntarily by Members of the Confraternity, is to learn by heart, each day, one sentence of the *Gayan*, until the entire book has been committed to memory. When the member can inform his seraj that he has done this, the sacred distinction of the name *Gayani* will be conferred upon him by the seraj-un-munir.

He may then proceed in the same manner with the *Vadan*, and if he succeeds in learning this book also, the sacred distinction of the name of *Vadani* will be conferred upon him by the seraj-un-munir.

Note. It is not necessary that the books be learnt in such a way that any part can be remembered at any time, although this should be the ideal before the one who undertakes this sacred task; but each verse must be learnt thoroughly at the time when it is studied.

The Knighthood of Purity

Spiritual chivalry is a Sufi tradition traced back to the prophet Abraham. In 1926, before returning to India, Hazrat Inayat Khan created four Knights of Purity (*Sahib(at) as-Safa*) and eight Heralds of the Message (*Naqib*). In 2010, the year of the hundredth jubilee of Sufism in the West, Shaikh al-Mashaik Mahmood Khan and Pir Zia Inayat-Khan established the Knighthood of Purity anew. The Knighthood of Purity is now composed of six degrees: Grand Master, Knight of Purity, Golden Herald, Silver Herald, Copper Herald, and Iron Herald.

All who seek to study and practice Murshid's philosophy and art of life, whether Sufi initiates or not, are eligible to receive the squirely designation of Iron Herald. Designation is by application to the Chancery.

Upon designation, the task of the Iron Herald is to recite the Iron Rules and to apply their morals in daily life. Each Rule is recited once a day, in the morning, over a forty-day period. The completion of the set of ten thus takes 400 days.

The Iron Herald is to notify the Chancellor upon completing the Iron Rules. He or she may then receive the squirely designation of Copper Herald and commence the recitation and practice of the Copper Rules. This procedure is repeated at the completion of each of the remaining sets of Rules. If no days are missed, the completion of all four sets takes 1600 days (four years and 140 days).

When all forty Rules have been recited and practiced for forty days each, the Golden Herald is qualified to receive, upon invitation, the accolade of Knight of Purity.

The Dargahs and the Hope Project

In the autumn of 1926, Hazrat Inayat Khan departed for India, attended by the Dutch mureed Kismet Stam. Arriving in Karachi, he traveled to Lahore and onward to New Delhi, where he took up residence in a house by the Yamuna River, known as Tilak Lodge. In the months that followed he spoke at the University of New Delhi, paid visits to Khwaja Hasan Nizami and Swami Shraddhanand, and made excursions by train to Lucknow, Agra, Benares, Jaipur, Ajmer, and Baroda.

Once, as Murshid was descending the steps of the Great Mosque in the old city, a dervish rushed toward him, excitedly saying, "I have been called to the Court, I have been called to the Court!" Murshid said afterward, "I shall soon know what it means."

On returning to Delhi following a brief visit to Baroda, Murshid fell ill. His condition took a serious turn on the night of February 4th. On the morning of the 5th, at twenty minutes past eight, his soul left his body.

Kismet writes, "In the evening following the passing of Murshid, a tremendous thunderstorm made the houses tremble. From all sides of the horizon lightning came, and flashed without ceasing for a long, long time."[1]

---

1 Kismet Stam, *Rays* (The Hague: East-West Publications, n.d.), p. 144.

When Kismet informed Khwaja Hasan Nizami of Murshid's death, he recalled that when Murshid had visited his home, which stood near the dargah of Hazrat Nizam ad-Din, Murshid had confided, "this place draws me." Accordingly, Nizami offered a portion of his land to serve as Murshid's final resting place.

Murshid's family visited Delhi two years later and constructed a tomb. When the grave was opened, despite the absence of a casket or any manner of embalming, Murshid's mortal remains were found to be miraculously preserved.

In later decades the Sufi Movement established a Memorial Trust and erected a spacious dargah over the tomb, with yellow dome and windows of filigreed white marble. The shrine is surrounded by a well-ordered complex consisting of a courtyard, lecture hall, school of music, library, retreat chambers, and caretaker's house.

Every year on February 5th, Murshid's *'Urs* (death anniversary) is celebrated at the dargah with prayers, Universal Worship, music, and the conveyance of a *chaddar* (a scented and embroidered sheet) from the dargah of Hazrat Nizam ad-Din. Pilgrims from across the world gather to lay rose petals on Murshid's tomb and imbibe the perfume of its atmosphere.

The urban village of Basti Hazrat Nizam ad-Din is a place of hallowed heritage, but also of dire poverty and the many problems that poverty breeds. Moved by the plight of the dwellers in the slums near the dargah, in 1980 Pir Vilayat founded an initiative to provide milk to undernourished mothers and children. The distribution of food at the dargahs of Sufi saints is an established tradition, but what distinguished this project, as it grew year by year, was its goal of helping the poor to help themselves. Today the Hope Project runs a health center, a crèche, a school, and a variety of vocational training programs.

The Hope Project is sustained by contributions from mureeds throughout the world. Many mureeds come to lend a hand for varying lengths of time. The Hope Project also attracts numerous workers from other charitable organizations, who come to receive training.

When Pir Vilayat died in 2004, he was buried in a plot of land adjoining the school of the Hope Project. Each year on June 17th, the day of his 'Urs, mureeds gather in remembrance at his dargah.

The Federation of the Sufi Message

During the lifetime of Hazrat Inayat Khan, the Sufi Movement remained a unified whole. After his passing, however,
differences arose and the original unity of the Movement was
sundered. As a result, the last century has seen the appearance
of multiple orders and organizations tracing their lineage to
Hazrat Inayat Khan. This process of division has been difficult at times, and has required lineage-bearing leaders and
communities to seek balance between fidelity to their own
lineage of transmission and tolerance for other perspectives
and adaptations.

The Federation of the Sufi Message was formed in 1997
to create an open space for fellowship and cooperation between mureeds of all orders and organizations identifying
with the Sufism of Hazrat Inayat Khan. The current member
organizations are the International Sufi Movement, the Sufi
Order International, the Sufi Ruhaniat International, Soefi
Contact, and the Fraternity of Light. The primary activity
of the Federation is an annual retreat hosted by the member organizations on a rotating basis in Europe and North
America.

Sulūk Academy

Sulūk Academy was established in 2002 with the mission of providing training in the Esoteric School for mureeds of all lineages traced to Hazrat Inayat Khan. The primary offering of Sulūk Academy is a two-year Core Course comprising forty days of study divided into four sections: Concentration, Contemplation, Meditation, and Realization. Graduates of the Core Course, known as "Wayfarers on the Endless Path" (*Salik(a) fi sabili'Llah*), are eligible to participate in specialized graduate studies focusing on the history, teachings, and practices of the Chishtiyya, Murshid's teachings and practices, and the teachings and practices of Pir Vilayat.

The central campus of Sulūk Academy is the Abode of the Message in New Lebanon, New York. Courses are also offered on the West Coast of the United States and in Europe.

Murshid's Blessing

May your heart be filled with heavenly joy,
May your soul be illuminated with divine light,
May your spirit uphold the divine Message,
May you go on in the spiritual path,
May God's peace abide with you for ever and evermore.[1]

1 *Complete Works of Pir-o-Murshid Hazrat Inayat Khan; Original Texts:
Sayings Part II* (London and The Hague: East-West Publications and
the Nekbakht Foundation, 1989), p. 202.

Hazrat Pir-o-Murshid Inayat Khan

Shaikh-ul-Mashaikh Maheboob Khan

Pir-o-Murshid Mohammed Ali Khan

Pir-o-Murshid Musharaff Khan

Murshida Rabia Martin

Murshida Sharifa Goodenough

Murshida Sophia Saintsbury-Green

Murshida Fazal Mai Egeling

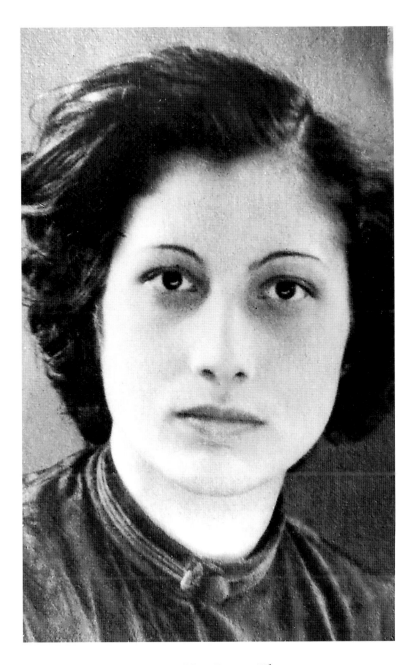

Noor-un-Nisa Inayat Khan

Pir Vilayat Inayat Khan

Sufi Ahmed Murad Chishti

Fazal Manzil and the cornerstone of the Universel, with the Mureeds' House in the background, Suresnes, France

Dargah of Hazrat Inayat Khan
New Delhi

Glossary of Names and Terms

akasha (Sanskrit): "sky"; in Sufism, an accommodation

'Ali, Hazrat: 'Ali ibn Abi Talib (d. 661), cousin and son-in-law
of the Prophet Muhammad

amal (*'amal*, Arabic): "work"; an advanced Sufi practice

Amir: Amir Ahmad Mina'i (d. 1900), a distinguished poet
and scholar of Lucknow

amma (Urdu): mother

'arsh (Arabic): "throne," the spiritual center in the forehead

'arsh al-'azam (Arabic): "great throne," the spiritual center at
the top of the head

asman (Persian): "sky"; in Sufism, an accommodation

baqa (Arabic): "subsistence"; the stage following *fana*

baraka (Arabic): blessing

bayat (bay'at, Arabic): "pledge"; initiation

begum (Urdu): lady

bhagwa (Urdu): ochre; color of garments worn by Hindu
ascetics and Chishti Sufis

bodhisattva (Sanskrit): in Buddhism, an enlightened being

chaddar (Urdu): sheet; in Sufism, a scented and embroidered
sheet for draping over a tomb

cherag (*chiragh*, Persian): "lamp"; an officiant of the Universal
Worship (fem. *cheraga*)

Chishti: of the Chishti Order, founded in Chisht, Afghanistan, and
introduced in India by Khwaja Mu'in ad-Din Hasan Sijzi-Ajmiri
Chishti

Chishtiyya: the Chishti Order

dargah (Persian): "court"; in Sufism, the tomb of a saint

dharma (Sanskrit): duty

fana (Arabic): annihilation

fazal (*fazl*, Urdu): "excess," grace; in Sufism, a word recited
as a blessing

Fazal Mai (*Fazl Mai*, Urdu): Mother of Grace

Fazal Manzil (*Fazl Manzil*, Urdu): House of Grace

fikar (*fikr,* Urdu): "thought"; in Sufism, contemplation

Gathas: the first series of Hazrat Inayat Khan's esoteric papers

Gathekas: a series of introductory papers by Hazrat Inayat
Khan

Gayan: the first collection of Hazrat Inayat Khan's sayings,
poems, and prayers

Gayatri (Sanskrit): "prayer"; the prayers of Hazrat Inayat
Khan

Githas: the second series of Hazrat Inayat Khan's esoteric
papers

Hadith (Arabic): "tradition," the collected sayings of the
Prophet Muhammad

hadith (Arabic): "tradition," a saying of the Prophet
Muhammad

Hahut (Arabic): the transcendent plane

halqa (Arabic): "circle"; a circle of Sufis

ijazat (Persian): certificate of authorization

Jabarut (Arabic): the spiritual plane

jamiat (jam'iyat, Persian): assembly

Jataka tales: a collection of stories describing the lives of the
Buddha in a variety of human and animal forms

Ka'ba: a cubical building in Mecca of ancient and enduring sanctity

Kafi, al- (Arabic): the All-Sufficient, a name of God

kalam (Arabic): "pen"; the spiritual center at the base of the spine

kefayat (*kifayat*, Persian): "sufficiency"; a senior title in Spiritual Healing

khalif(a) (*khalifa*, Arabic): "successor"; a senior title in the Esoteric School

khandan (Urdu): household

khankah (*khanqah*, Urdu): Sufi headquarters

Khatum: a prayer of Hazrat Inayat Khan

Khizr, Khwaja: the Green Man of Islam, guide of Moses and of numerous saints

kursi (Arabic): "seat"; the spiritual center in the chest

Lahut (Arabic): the divine plane

lauh (Arabic): "tablet"; the spiritual center in the abdomen

madar-ul-maham (*madaru'l-mahamm*, Urdu): "center of affairs"; Secretary General of the Esoteric School

Malakut (Arabic): the mental plane

manan (Sanskrit): in Vedanta, reflection

maulana (Urdu): a learned doctor

Murad Hasil (Persian): "wish attained"; the name given by Hazrat Inayat Khan to a place in Katwijk, The Netherlands

mureed (*murid*, Persian): "willing"; a Sufi initiate; a title in the Esoteric School

murshid (Persian): "guide"; a senior title in the Esoteric School (fem. *murshida*) *murshidzade* (Persian): son of the murshid

murshidzadi (Persian): daughter of the murshid

nabi (Arabic): prophet

nafs (Arabic): self, ego

namaz (Persian): prayer

Nasut (Arabic): the physical plane

Nayaz: a prayer of Hazrat Inayat Khan

Nirtan: the third collection of sayings, poems, and prayers by Hazrat Inayat Khan

noor (*nur*, Arabic): light

pir (Persian): spiritual director

pirani (Urdu): female pir, or wife of the pir

pirzade (Persian): son of the pir

pirzadi (Persian): daughter of the pir

pir-o-murshid (Persian): "spiritual director and guide"; the most senior title in the Esoteric School

prana (Sanskrit): life force

Prophet, the: Abu'l-Qasim Muhammad ibn ʿAbd Allah (d. 632), the "seal of the prophets"

qasab (*kasb*, Arabic): "acquisition"; in Sufism, a breathing practice

raga (Sanskrit): a melodic mode in Indian music

Ram Nam (Sankrit): "the name Rama"; a Hindu chant

rasul (Arabic): messenger, prophet

risalat (Arabic): the prophetic mission

rind (Persian): "rogue"; an unorthodox mystic

Rumi: Jalal ad-Din Muhammad Balkhi (d. 1273), famed Persian Sufi poet of Konya

Sa'di: Abu Muhammad Muslih ad-Din bin 'Abd Allah Shirazi (d. 1291), famed Persian Sufi poet of Shiraz

Sahaba-yi Safa (Persian): Knights of Purity, an epithet of the early Sufis

Salat: a prayer of Hazrat Inayat Khan

salik (Arabic): traveler on the spiritual path

sama' (Arabic): "audition"; the Sufi practice of listening to music

samadhi (Sanskrit): non-dual consciousness

Sangathas: the third series of Hazrat Inayat Khan's esoteric papers

Sangithas: the fourth series of Hazrat Inayat Khan's esoteric papers

Saum: a prayer of Hazrat Inayat Khan

seraj (*siraj*, Arabic): "lamp"; a senior title in the Universal Worship (fem. *seraja*)

seraj-un-munir (*sirajun munir*, Arabic): "shining lamp"; the most senior title in the Universal Worship

Shafi, ash- (Arabic): the Healer, a name of God

shagal (*shughl*, Arabic): "occupation"; a Sufi breathing practice

shaikh (Arabic): spiritual director; a senior title in the Esoteric School

shaikh-ul-mashaikh (*shaikh al-masha'ikh*, Arabic): "shaikh of shaikhs"; an alternative form of the senior-most title in the Esoteric School

shefayat (*shifa'at*, Arabic): "intercession"; a title in Spiritual Healing

Siddiq: Abu Bakr Siddiq (d. 634), the first successor of the Prophet Muhammad in Sunni Islam

sushupti (Sanskrit): dreamless sleep

talib (Arabic): seeker

taran (Sanskrit): swimming, deliverance

tawajjuh (Arabic): "attention"; in Sufism, the spiritual influence of the pir

turiyavastha (*turiya avastha*, Sanskrit): pure consciousness

urs (*'urs,* Urdu): "marriage feast"; the death anniversary of a Sufi saint

Vedanta: the Hindu texts known as the Upanishads; also, the philosophy originating from them

Vedas: the most ancient collection of Indian sacred texts

wazifa (Arabic): "task"; in Sufism, a daily recitation

zamindar (Persian): feudal landowner

Zend Avesta: the primary sacred texts of the Zoroastrian religion

zikar (*zikr,* Persian): "remembrance"; in Sufism, the ritual of divine remembrance

ziraat (*zira'at,* Persian): "agriculture": an activity of the Sufi Movement

Works by Hazrat Inayat Khan

Musicological works

Balasan Gitmala
Sayaji Garbawali
Inayat Git Ratnawali
Inayat Harmonium Shikshak
Inayat Fidal Shikshak
Minqar-i Musiqar

Sufi works

1914   *A Sufi Message of Spiritual Liberty*
1915   *The Confessions of Inayat Khan*
1918   *A Sufi Prayer of Invocation*
        Hindustani Lyrics
        Songs of India
        The Divan of Inayat Khan
        Akibat
1919   *Love, Human and Divine*
        The Phenomenon of the Soul
        Pearls from the Ocean Unseen
1921   *In an Eastern Rosegarden*
1922   *The Way of Illumination*
        The Message
1923   *The Inner Life*
        The Mysticism of Sound
        Notes from the Unstruck Music from the Gayan Manuscript
        The Alchemy of Happiness
1924   *The Soul—Whence and Whither*
1926   *The Divine Symphony, or Vadan*

Posthumous Sufi works

1927   *The Purpose of Life*
1928   *The Unity of Religious Ideals*
1931   *Health*
        Character Building; The Art of Personality

1934   *Education*
1935   *The Mind World*
       Yesterday, Today, and Tomorrow
1936   *The Solution of the Problem of the Day*
1937   *Cosmic Language*
       Moral Culture
1938   *Rassa Shastra: The Science of Life's Creative Forces*
1939   *Three Plays*
       Metaphysics: the Experience of the Soul in Different Planes of Existence

Collected works

1960–67 *The Sufi Message of Hazrat Inayat Khan,* 12 vols.
1988–   *Complete Works of Pir-o-Murshid Hazrat Inayat Khan: Original Texts,* 11 vols. (to date)

Works about Hazrat Inayat Khan

Bloch, Regina Miriam. *The Confessions of Inayat Khan*. London: The Sufi Publication Society, 1915. (Reprinted in *The Sufi Message*, vol. 12)

De Jong-Keesing, Elisabeth. *Inayat Khan: A Biography*. The Hague: East-West Publications, 1974.

   Inayat Answers. London and The Hague: Fine Books Oriental and East-West Publications, 1977.

Guillaume-Schamhart, Elise, and Van Voorst van Beest, Munira, ed. *The Biography of Pir-o-Murshid Inayat Khan*. The Hague: East-West Publications, 1979.

Inayat Khan, Pir Vilayat. *The Message in Our Time: The Life and Teachings of the Sufi Master Pir-o-Murshid Inayat Khan*. San Francisco: Harper & Row, 1979.

Inayat-Khan, Pirzade Zia, ed., *A Pearl in Wine: Essays in the Life, Music, and Sufism of Hazrat Inayat Khan*. New Lebanon: Omega Publications, 2001.

Khan, Inayat. *The Story of My Mystical Life*. The Hague: East-West Publications, 1982.

Khan, Musharaff Moulamia. *Pages in the Life of a Sufi*. The Hague: East-West Publications, 1982.

Saintsbury-Green, Sophia. *Images of Inayat*. New Lebanon, NY: Omega Publications, 1992).

Stam, Kismet Dorothea. *Rays*. The Hague: East-West Publications, n.d.

Van Beek, Wil. *Hazrat Inayat Khan: Master of Life, Modern Sufi Mystic*. New York: Vantage Press, 1983.

Van Hoorn, Theo. *Recollections of Inayat Khan and Western Sufism*. Translated, annotated, and introduced by Hendrik J. Horn. Leiden: Foleor Publishers, 2010.

Van Stolk, Sirkar, and Dunlop, Daphne. *Memories of a Sufi Sage: Hazrat Inayat Khan*. East-West Publications, 1975.

Works about Sufism

Dowland, Nargis. *At the Gate of Discipleship*. Southampton, England: The Sufi Movement, n.d.

Between the Desert and the Sown: The Way of the Disciple. Southampton, England: The Sufi Movement, n.d.

The Lifted Veil. Southampton, England: The Sufi Movement, 1925.

Goodenough, Sharifa. *Soufisme d'Occident*. Paris: La Colombe, 1962.

Inayat Khan, Hidayat. *The Inner School: Esoteric Sufi Teachings*. Vancouver, B.C.: Ekstasis Editions, 1996.

Inayat Khan, Pir Vilayat. *That Which Transpires Behind That Which Appears*. New Lebanon: Omega Publications, 1994.

In Search of the Hidden Treasure. New York: J.P. Tarcher/ Putnam, 2003.

The Ecstasy Beyond Knowing. (Forthcoming: Sulūk Press/ Omega Publications, 2014)

Jironet, Dr. Karin. *Sufi Mysticism into the West: Life and Leadership of Hazrat Inayat Khan's Brothers, 1927–1967.* Leuven, Belgium: Peeters, 2009.

Lewis, Samuel L. *In the Garden.* New York: Harmony Books, 1975.

Mona, M.C. *Short Dictionary of the Foreign Words in Hazrat Inayat Khan's Teachings.* Alkmaar, The Netherlands: Stichting Bewustzijn, 1991.

Saintsbury-Green, Sophia. *The Wings of the World: The Sufi Message as I see It.* Deventer, Holland, and London: A.E. Kluwer and Luzac & Co., 1934.

Memories of Hazrat Inayat Khan by a Disciple. London: Rider and Co., n.d.

Van Tuyll, H.P. *Prayer, Meditation, Silence.* The Hague: East-West Publications, 1998.

Witteveen, Dr. H.J. *Universal Sufism.* Shaftesbury, Dorset: Element, 1997.

Contributors

Shrabani Basu is a journalist and historian. She is the author of *Spy Princess; The Life of Noor Inayat Khan*. Her other books include *Victoria & Abdul; The True Story of the Queen's Closest Confidant* and *Curry; The Story of the Nation's Favourite Dish*. She set up the Noor Inayat Khan Memorial Trust in 2010 and led a high-profile campaign to install a personal memorial in London for Noor Inayat Khan. The memorial was unveiled on 8 November, 2012, by Princess Anne.

Nargis Dowland (d. 1953) ran the Polygon House Hotel in Southampton, England. She became a mureed in 1919 and was made National Representative of England in 1921. She authored three books elaborating the teachings of Hazrat Inayat Khan: *Between the Desert and the Sown*, *The Gate of Discipleship*, and *The Lifted Veil*.

Dr. Sitara Jironet is a Sufi and a Jungian psychoanalyst. She is co-founder of In Claritas, a community of scholars, artists and business leaders exploring the global image of future governance. She is also Executive Committee Officer of the Dutch Association of Analytical Psychology and the author of numerous articles and five books, including *Sufi Mysticism into the West: Life and Leadership of Hazrat Inayat Khan's Brothers 1927–1967* and *The Image of Spiritual Liberty in the Sufi Movement Following Hazrat Inayat Khan*.

Murshid Wali Ali Meyer is a Sufi teacher, editor and writer. He served as Murshid Samuel Lewis' esoteric secretary and edited many of his manuscripts for publication. Wali Ali co-authored *Physicians of the Heart: A Sufi View of the 99 Names of Allah*. He is the head of the Esoteric School of the Sufi Ruhaniat International and the director of Khankah S.A.M. in San Francisco.

Huzurnavaz baron van Pallandt (1903–1977) was a Dutch diplomat and editor of the twelve-volume collection *The Sufi Message of Hazrat Inayat Khan*. His biography of Hazrat Inayat Khan, included in this book in abridged form, was issued as a supplement to that series.

Pir Zia Inayat-Khan is a scholar and teacher of Sufism in the lineage of his grandfather, Hazrat Inayat Khan. He received his B.A. (Hons) in Persian Literature from the London School of Oriental and African Studies, and his M.A. and Ph.D. in Religion from Duke University. Pir Zia is president of the Sufi Order International and founder of Suluk Academy, a school of contemplative study with branches in the United States and Europe. He is also founder of the interspiritual institute Seven Pillars House of Wisdom. He lives with his wife and two children in rural upstate New York.

Index

A

abdomen 122–123, 213

Abode of the Message 75, 194

Abraham 12, 83, 134, 175, 188

air 50, 101, 128–129, 137

Ajmer 45, 75, 190

akasha 121–122, 184, 211. *See also asman*

alchemy 76

'Ali, Hazrat: 'Ali ibn Abi Talib 20, 27–28, 30–33, 211

Allah 25, 28–33, 63, 78, 101–102, 115–116, 126–127, 221 . *See also* God

'amal 115

Amir, Ahmad Mina'i 21, 211

angel 20, 75, 148, 163

annihilation 21, 42, 106, 115–116, 212. *See also fana*

Arabia 25

Arab(ic) 3, 42, 79, 108, 211–216

'arsh 123, 211

'arsh al-'Azam 123, 211

art 13, 40, 105, 167: art of life 188

asman 122, 211. *See also akasha*

attainment 10–12, 15, 59, 99, 101, 148

attitude 9–10, 37, 58, 91, 133, 146, 148, 167

B

balance 91, 121, 149, 193

Balasan Gitmala 40, 217

baqa 42, 102, 211

baqa bi'Llah 102, 116

baraka 78. *See also* blessing, *fazal*

Baroda 39–42, 54–55, 57, 190

Basti Hazrat Nizam ad-Din 191, 209. *See also* Nizam ad-Din Mahbub-i Ilahi Badauni Chishti

bayat 86, 99. *See also* initiation

beauty 9, 19, 37, 40–42, 48–49, 72, 99, 102, 105, 133–135, 137, 147, 152, 171, 174–175, 179

belief 7–8, 11, 59, 83, 100, 149, 169–170; believer 75, 104. *See also* creed, faith, religion

beloved 12, 102; Beloved, the divine 9, 19, 105–106, 137, 151–152. *See also* God

Besant, Annie 65

Bhayaji 57

Bible 14. *See also* Jesus Christ, Old Testament, Peter, individual prophets by name

blessing 4, 12, 25, 38, 50, 125, 135–136, 173, 176, 195. *See also baraka, fazal*

bodhisattva 14, 211

body 7, 21, 57, 71, 105, 107–108, 115, *(cont. overleaf)*

225